Cocaine

Murder In The 1st Degree

BORROWED TIME!

Edgar Vernell Futrell Jr.

ISBN: 9798300708917

Dedication

Remembering with love my dear mother, Hattie Futrell, and my cherished father, Edgar Futrell Sr.

CONTENTS

About the Author

My name is Edgar Futrell, and I am a college grad majoring in psychology and sociology. I underwent some extremely hard times as a terrible teen; I mistakenly thought I knew my way, but I was far from the real world. Falling off the high road onto the low was a very painful experience I will never forget. Twenty-one years after my release from prison, I have become an entrepreneur and have dedicated my gym time to working with at-risk youth, juvenile delinquents, and kids who suffer from mental disorders on all levels because they are those unsuspecting children who will walk into a school with an A K assault weapon and kills 20 students. My goal is to intervene to interrupt their thinking.

In part, my time spent in prison was the majority responsible for the crafting of this book, thinking outside the box; this awesome suspenseful drama will have you scratching your head and turning to your last page before you can solve the mystery. Secondly, my goal is to open a door in the mental health field that's slowly beginning to open because people are quietly suffering, and that disorder can only lead to a "dangerous" situation.

Thomas Edison best showcased his positive thinking when he saw that the cup was half full and that anything was possible when he invented the light bulb, which still lights the entire world today. His positive thinking says that if you could harness the human brain for just 24 hours, you would have generated enough power to light the entire city in which you live for one year.

The Red Light Machete Bandit will blow your mind when he
lights the city with his Red Light fetus.

Page Blank Intentionally

Chapter 1

Gut-Wrenching! Suspenseful!

The Red-Light Machete Bandit was the insane parachutist who had jumped from a plane without a parachute or safety net—a daredevil on full charge. A kleptomaniac is notorious for catching flashy drug dealers at red-light intersections while they were flaunting their wealth. For instance, The Ice Man was flamboyant and flashy with his extravagant jewelry ensemble, sporting a Cadillac on 24s. His hand gestures were animated at the red light intersection, strongly suggesting, without hearing the language, "He's the big boss in this place!"

Suddenly, a strange chill surged through the air. Abruptly, he stopped waving his arm. Out of nowhere, a psychotic lunatic approached the truck with a machete, mutilating his hand. In that instant, everything stood still—temporarily paralyzed. With the whole world spinning on its axis, the only thing the bandit said was:

"It's like that!"

The Red Light Machete Bandit snatched up the bloody hand and, like magic, faded into the landscape as he swiftly ran through a backyard, eluding the police. The police and ambulance arrived immediately on the scene. The poor woman in the car behind witnessed the chilling scene as it unfolded, cringing in shock, terrified, as she watched this hopeless man get robbed of his hand. He had been carrying a gun, and in such shock, he forgot he even had it. All he could do was frantically try to retrieve his hand.

The police department and news media immediately came out of nowhere. It had all happened so fast.

"I know walls have ears!" someone remarked. "When you think no one's watching, the whole world has you center stage, waiting to applaud your best or condemn your worst unscrupulous performance."

The machete bandit had sent the entire police force in all metropolitan areas—from the lowest ranking to the highest—into a frenzy. They were baffled, looking for informants to help track this deranged person down ASAP. The police were getting phone calls from the highest branch of government to the lowest.

"This is bananas! One person can change the course of the city in a flash?" someone questioned.

The state and federal government agencies knew that if this person wasn't captured quickly, he could commit another random act of violence and take another arm, finger, or life. People were calling the media out of fear, panicking, in an attempt to get the media involved with the story through their immense concerns about not feeling safe in traffic.

"This guy is cutting off arms, hands, and fingers. What's next? An ankle bracelet? Snatching people out of cars and strangling them? I am petrified to be threatened and terrorized at the same time!" a resident exclaimed.

No one knew when or who would be next on his hit list or where he'd pop up. He had no specific area he targeted. After the public poured their concerns into the media's hands, they acted swiftly to get the ball rolling. When the story blew up, the police chief constructed a special task force, the "Crime Gurus."

"Operation Shutdown" was classified as elite, with a plausible, cunning edge that complemented their impeccable style; they knew exactly how to break a case down. But this guy was more than mystical. He knew precisely how to shake the police. His homeboys knew he was uncanny, deranged, and delusional in his head.

"It's hilarious to them," some observed, "considering they weren't the brightest color in the box."

The Red Light Machete Bandit had become the main subject, with pun intended, in every household for breakfast, lunch, and dinner. Some lower-class citizens laughed in ignorance, while the upper class wept in fear.

"Am I next on his blacklist?" a concerned citizen wondered. "This is unbelievable!"

There was more to this story. Mayor Michael Bloomberg had laid off 167 police officers one week ago, citing downsizing as the rationale. The manhunt to capture the bandit wreaked havoc statewide. Panic raced across the state faster than a telephone call! Twenty police officers were called back to work.

The Red Light Machete Bandit had lost his right arm to a drug lord, but that didn't stop him. The police did the honors of naming this ridiculously horrifying person the "Red Light Machete Bandit" to be able to distinguish him from other foul criminals. His spree continued! The following day, he was back on the prowl, trying to meet another quota. The more cocaine he consumed, the more he wanted. Addicts always needed more to achieve that euphoric feeling. Dope fiends were dangerously infatuated with that temporary band-aid that rid the pain.

There were always horrifying stories resting inside the minds of those living in the magical world of cocaine. Mike and his partner had been rolling through the hood on a calm sunny day, enjoying the scenery, when he noticed the signal light turning yellow. He slowed down, finally coming to a complete stop. Behind them was a young player, "Zip Down," a beast in the streets, flashing his fancy jewelry, attracting all the young cuties with his over-the-top swagger. The brother was popping his collar!

"I couldn't resist staring in my rearview mirror," Mike admitted. "A class act! He really puts on a show."

All of a sudden, just before the light changed, Mike saw the one-armed guy run up to the car behind him very quickly, hurling a machete over his head. Down it came, cutting Zip's hand completely off. Zip jerked back like a dog had bitten his hand.

"Dang, man!" Mike shouted.

He immediately told his partner, Jerry, to look, but it had happened so incredibly fast that the only thing Jerry saw was the one-armed guy running away.

"It looked like he put the machete in a pouch and tucked the goods underneath his bad arm, then ran like a bat out of hell," Jerry said.

At that precise moment, Police Officer Collins had been surveying an alley notorious for criminals' rite of passage, with one hour left before ending his shift. Just as he came to the end of the alley, observing traffic, he glanced to his right and saw the Red Light Machete Bandit cut off another victim's hand at the intersection. A lady had been watching frantically from a third-floor apartment, witnessing almost the entire ordeal. She saw the bandit cut off the hand at the red light and puked simultaneously. Then, she saw the police officer in pursuit of the perpetrator in front of her apartment, but unfortunately, she lost sight of them as they disappeared to the side of the apartment. Officer Collins stated that the perpetrator had run through the backyard and vanished.

He held up at the rear of an apartment complex. As soon as Officer Collins grabbed the fence, attempting to jump over and pressing his weight on it before leaping to the other side, he felt something hard hit his hand, causing him to lose balance and tumble to the other side, rolling into a fetal position from the excruciating pain he had sustained. He knew he had to get to his feet quickly and make it to the hospital if he wanted to save his hand. He noticed clothing hanging on a line, snatched a T-shirt to tie around his arm to slow the blood flow, then picked up his hand and ran back to his car. As the officer came back through the gangway, the eyewitness in the apartment saw him carrying his bloody hand. She was so shaken her bottom jaw dropped. The officer rushed to the hospital with his siren roaring for passage.

When he arrived, the doctor asked, "What happened to you?"

The Red Light Machete Bandit's dopehead partner, Larry, waited until he returned with the jewelry to sell it to the underworld crime boss "Big Squeeze," who was notorious for buying drug dealers' jewelry and melting it down. Big Squeeze owned a funeral home. He stole jewelry from the dead. No one knew.

"Who opens the coffin once they're at the cemetery?" Big Squeeze would say. "It's a done deal. Wow! Rewind that! Steal from the dead..."

"Yeah! Dang, man, that's deep," Larry replied.

Big Squeeze looked at the hand. "You cut off the wrong hand this time. This is Zip's ring. You should have gone ahead and cut his throat because that's a dangerous dude. You know he's going to send his bloodhounds out to hunt you down. I'll still take it because I'm only going to have it melted down."

The bandit's timing had been good, with everyone being allowed to wear masks because of COVID-19. This was an excellent opportunity for Larry to execute his plan. Nobody looked out of place wearing a mask.

One week later, the Red Light Machete Bandit was working around Club Onyx when he noticed a well-known baller, Big Mike's car. Mike had been trying to clean his dirty money by turning rapper while still slinging his drugs to get studio time and other luxuries. He hung out at the club quite frequently. He and his girlfriend had been spotted leaving the club, walking towards Mike's car. Mike had been too inebriated to drive, so his girlfriend, a preacher's kid, decided to play it safe and drive them home. They both were competitive in the jewelry department, flaunting so hard it could blind someone. Mike got in on the passenger side and slumped down in the seat, lighting up a blunt. At that same time, his girlfriend's arm was hanging outside the window, and she was caught by the Red Light Machete Bandit. He whacked her hand off, laughing as he ran in a zigzag across the street, taking the $5,000 bracelet and $10,000 in rings, fading into the scenery as though nothing had happened. Patricia unconsciously pressed on the gas, running into a store. The police happened to be on sight and retrieved her hand, thereafter rushing her to the hospital.

Larry eventually took a time out and went to prison. His friend Ghost lost his foot on Riker's Island because he loved downers. One day, Ghost came up with a crazy notion to inject spit into his foot to make it swell to get pain medication. He figured it would definitely get him a lay-in from work. Boy, did it surprise him when it swelled to the size of an elephant's foot! When he went to the doctor for X-rays, it was determined there was no chance of saving his foot.

His foot was amputated. Now, he was disabled, relying on the government's care packages once a month. The Red Light Machete Bandit continued visiting his friend in the hospital because the infection was traveling up his leg to his heart.

"Murphy's Law is a bitch!" he said. "What can happen, will happen!"

In Larry's world, people were crawling on their bellies 24/7 like snakes, and they couldn't be trusted. It was like imagining untamed lions out of their habitat, free to roam, terrorizing and sucking the life out of people like a human vacuum. Both young and old hustlers were notorious for wearing a mask to prevent disclosure.

In that world, the rule was, "Never reveal your true identity."

Larry never quite understood that theory because criminals always left DNA somewhere.

"You never know when someone's going to 'paint' on you," he said, meaning snitch.

When people got caught, their minds raced faster than the speed of light, figuring out an angle to cushion the seemingly endless fall into a bottomless pit of fire. As they continued falling, they thought about eerie stories that Larry used to boast about—stories that could have been used to save a misguided child's life. Unfortunately, that was not the case.

"Anyway," Larry muttered, "his first day out of orientation, he was sent to a housing unit in general population with some young fools."

"Walk with me if you dare through the prison gates of pure hell," he would say, "to learn the most disgusting prison secrets that rest in the cracks of the walls, private journals kept secret by corrupt wardens, guards, and inmates!"

Through the windows of Larry's mind, others would learn the terrifying, untold stories that would make their hearts quiver as tears flowed uncontrollably. Larry met a young kid, sixteen years old, named Lancaster—a cocaine, heroin, and weed addict with a drinking disorder and other cringing character flaws.

He had been certified as an adult by the juvenile courts for stealing a car that ultimately landed him in prison for accidentally killing a pedestrian walking up the exit ramp off the freeway at night. He pleaded guilty and got twenty years. In his struggle for freedom, he visited the law library to seek paralegal assistance.

At the first desk sat this big, robust guy who obviously lifted weights.

"The guy looked like he could lift the whole gym!" Larry joked.

His AKA was Big Red. He greeted the youngster at the door.

"Red seems friendly and ingenious," Lancaster had said. He shook his hand and was encouraged to have a seat.

The kid, out the gate, told Red, "I need help to get back in court. How much will I be out of pocket?"

Big Red told him, "Blood, just give me ten boxes of cigarettes on a residual plan, and I'll see if I can make that happen for you!"

He took the case but with a hidden agenda. Almost everyone in prison wore masks—they were not who they said they were. Big Red filed his pro se motions.

"Now put on your skin diving gear to surf through the sour rubbish with me," Larry said, "to see what happens to youngsters who have no other choice but to act upon blind faith as they courageously walk through the shadows of darkness, fearing no evil that lurks!"

Sixty days later, the appeals court responded to Lancaster's writ, filed appealing his conviction. The judicial system acknowledged merit in his claim, scheduling a hearing date. He couldn't wait for doors to be unlocked so he could get to the library to share his good news with Big Red.

"Remember, initially, the agreement was ten boxes of cigarettes," Larry reminded.

When Lancaster got there, Red was with another client. Lancaster sat patiently waiting. When the client left, Red called him over to his desk.

Lancaster told him, "Man, you really know your stuff. I got a court date! But they asked questions I didn't understand."

The law clerk took a glimpse at the document, looked over his glasses, and said, "I can definitely get you out of here, but it's bigger than cigarettes."

Lancaster replied, "Call it, Red!"

Red leaned over to the kid with a harsh stare, rubbed his leg, and said, "A sexual favor will set you free."

The kid's dream was abruptly shattered. The overbearing assault surged to the central core of his heart, causing post-traumatic stress. His heart beat out of his chest like a bass drum, his blood pressure shot through the ceiling, and his teeth and fists were tightly clenched. Still, the worst was yet to come. What happened next was catastrophic. Lancaster was infuriated but had been taught not to wear his feelings on his sleeve. He knew the cost of making a scene, so he humbly left while creating a plan: "Kill that freak!"

He knew the risk taken when violating the underground constitutional law—the law that stipulated, before providing a knife to anyone, one must first know "who it's for." It didn't matter. On that rainy day, he had to take a chance in the dark; it was do or die.

He stumbled upon Little John, whom he had met in orientation. He hardly knew the guy but trusted him enough to tell him what had happened. John chuckled with a scandalous persona, as though the same heinous thing had happened to him.

John told Lancaster, "Man, I got you faded! I'm dying to see the dripping blood from the hands of the man who takes this big, bad mother's life."

Minutes later, Little John went to the library to tell Big Red the news on the vine: "Lancaster's looking for a knife to put you down."

Big Red gave Little John a box of cigarettes for the information and immediately put a hit out for twenty boxes of cigarettes.

Chapter 2

The next day, Lancaster was walking down the tunnel to chow when he was "V-necked" and stabbed to death. Asking for a knife in prison could backfire. Prison history strongly suggested that a convict out to screw you sexually was not going to assist you in your release from prison.

When the guards unlocked the doors, instead of Larry going to the library that day to study, he and Duke decided to go to the yard for recreation, just to get out of the cell. They sat in the bleachers discussing Lancaster's situation while watching the "A-league" handball players put down moves you wouldn't believe, smacking the ball between their legs, and watching inmates run track for hours nonstop.

Two hours later, an inmate quietly walked up behind them and stood at the very top of the bleachers, attentively staring at joggers as they gracefully ran. Suddenly, he lunged onto the field in pursuit of an exhausted jogger who was squeamishly panting for breath. Thirty miles nonstop was very good, but not good enough here. Suddenly, he slowed down. The guard in the tower thought nothing of it because inmates played all the time, blocking out the stress.

When the assailant caught the jogger, he slugged him over the head with an iron pipe. The jogger dropped like a log cut at the base. The beating continued for about twenty seconds. Snapping out of the moment, the assailant realized it was time to make his break and get to the other side of the prison to blend in with other inmates.

That same evening in the chow hall, Larry found out that Lancaster had been killed. At the same time he heard the bad news, a guy was horribly stabbed in the eye with a foot-long shank for sitting in someone's seat. The assailant continued stabbing him until he actually lost his breath. It wasn't until the prison guards assigned to kitchen duty asked the inmate, "Are you through? Can I have the knife?"

The inmate responded, "Hell no! Take me to the hole first!"

He stabbed the victim multiple times without balking and told the guard, "I'm not giving you s--t until I get to lock up!"

The guard escorted him to lock up.

Larry also told a ridiculous story of why inmates went to the guard shack pretending to get lighter fluid refills for lighters, when in fact, they saved it until acquiring enough to dash into an inmate's cell for revenge by burning him to death.

In prison, inmates decorated their cells with towels to avoid the constant reminder of being imprisoned. Towels on the lockers, walls, and bars. Now some crazy maniac with access to lighter fluid dashed it on your towels while you were trapped inside. The guards, conveniently distracted by a massive, staged outburst of loud noise calling for assistance on another tier, on a different floor, released the door to let you out. Guards couldn't be in all places at the same time. In the meantime, you were burning to death—a human death trap described it best.

"Criminals are awfully good on their feet when foxed in a corner," Larry said. "They're even smarter when caught red-handed with the smoking gun dangling from their index finger. In their world, 'right's not always right, and wrong's not always wrong.'"

The next day (Sunday), following Lancaster's death with spring two days away, miles away was an elderly African American woman with extraordinary charisma and phenomenal timeless beauty—Mrs. Martha Reid. She had two incredibly obnoxious grandchildren who could just smell themselves—spoiled rotten.

Their parents had been killed in a tragic car accident two years ago. The only thing left behind was a house with lien holders. Martha decided to do something that would be entertaining in her retirement. Most of her neighbors thought she was a genius with enormous wealth; instead, she was a loner with few relatives. She had a dream of someday owning a really nice home in an upscale neighborhood with lots of acres—grass as far as the eye could see—with incredibly fascinating activities for her entertainment.

While reading the weekly Sunday paper, scrolling through the real estate section, she noticed a beautiful, fully furnished condo at Pleasure Island Resort. It had acres of land surrounded by pretty evergreens and pine trees, with unimaginable entertainment for residents.

"Excited!" she thought.

She contacted the owner immediately before changing her mind to make arrangements to visit this extraordinary work of art and hopefully lease with an option to buy. Her intuition told her, "This is the one for me," so she followed her gut instinct.

The phone rang.

"Hello!" A vivacious voice answered.

"My name is Martha Reid. Can I speak with Mr. Banks, please?"

"Could you hold for a minute, please? I'll see if he's available."

A moment later, "Hello, Robert Banks speaking! How may I help you?"

"Mesmerized!" she thought.

"I noticed an ad in the Sunday paper describing the fabulous condos available," she said. "I am anxiously looking forward to a walk-through to see if it's ideally what I'm looking for. When is a good time to view the property?"

"Well, Mrs. Reid—"

"Call me Martha," she interrupted.

"Thanks," said Mr. Banks, who turned out to be insidious and diabolical. He continued, "It's ironic you called. I was just making arrangements for an open house tomorrow! How does that work for your schedule?"

"Well, I'm usually out of church by 11:00 am. How about 2:00 pm?" Martha replied.

"Wonderful, it's a date!" he answered.

When Martha arrived the next day, she noticed right away, "I'm the only potential customer here to view the property at 1111 Woodcrest Rd." She was extremely excited and impressed with the decor of the place.

"Fantastic! It was a picture-perfect dream come true," she thought.

While walking through the resort, observing all the very tastefully designed amenities—swimming pool, a movie theater, Jacuzzi, a horse trail, and golf course—she remarked, "I am so glad no one else showed up. I want this home."

Likewise, Mr. Banks read it in her eyes. She wore her feelings on her sleeve and he knew she would compromise with any offer tendered. He had her eating out of the palm of his hand. She couldn't wait to hit that loaded bank account. She was a really good candidate for the scheme he had in mind.

Mr. Banks had been under scrutiny by the DEA for quite some time due to suspected drug ring operations linked nationwide. He definitely was not a local boy with little experience. He had to find someone naive, with absolutely no motivation to circumvent drugs, not a clue. Someone that the task force wouldn't suspect involvement in, even in the next lifetime.

Inside the home, she discovered the fully furnished condo, with options to keep the furniture already installed or replace it.

There was a tall vintage cherry oak wood china cabinet, ideally crafted with secret compartments that she knew absolutely nothing about. Infatuated, she made the offer to buy the condo with the option to keep only the china cabinet in the home. Mr. Banks smiled with arrogance, a touch of humor covering his real, genuine concerns.

"This cabinet must cost ten thousand dollars," he thought.

It had remote-controlled hidden drawers where Mr. Banks stashed his drugs, which he could only access from another room connected to her home. The drawers opened from the back, built into the wall to prevent disclosure. Additionally, there were fake walls that slid across to conceal the drawers. Kilos of cocaine were stashed there all the time.

Martha loved sitting in the living room for hours, watching sports entertainment, political events, reading her journal, and playing the daily New York Stock Exchange with portions of her earnings from her "Snap Back Auto Insurance Co." It was an amazing way to amuse herself as a retired, self-made, extremely wealthy neurologist and a telepathic stock market guru. Martha knew exactly when to hold and when to fold.

One hot summer day, after being there for a while, she invited her great-grandkids and their friends to spend the vacation at her breathtaking fantasy home that anyone would envy in a positive, motivational kind of way.

Once they arrived, Grandma told them, "I'm not too crazy about my golf course because occasionally, a ball would rip through my window."

Banks had to maintain access to Martha's home because she unknowingly stored his drugs there. When his remote control failed to open the drawers to her china cabinet, where the drugs were kept, he would stage a high wind event causing a power outage. Sometimes, an occasional golf ball would find its way through her window, or he would make a courtesy check to ensure she was comfortable.

Mrs. Reid told her grandchildren, "I never paid any real attention to the temporary breakdowns or mishaps because they take care of it immediately! Mr. Banks is such a sweet person."

Her grandson Michael, however, was suspicious of Mr. Banks right away. He knew something wasn't quite right.

"A home of this magnitude in a secluded, remote area?" he thought. "The golfers appear to be semi-professionals. Why so many reckless shots through Grandma's window?"

Michael decided, "If this happens while I'm here, I am going to snoop around to see what's really going on."

Michael was a part-time thug on a small scale with licenses in carpentry and electrical work.

Cling!

"Oops, another golf ball!" he muttered.

Early Thursday morning, a golf ball broke the window again. Michael and his wife had stayed awake all night on the balcony, talking about how wonderful it must be to own a property like this. Just before daybreak, they had fallen asleep for a second—at least that's how it seemed. Those short naps were the hardest to pull yourself out of.

Opening his eyes, Michael saw a repairman carrying a large toolbox, inappropriate for a window repair. He told his best friend Jerry, who had come along to spend the summer at his grandma's house, as well as his sister Sherry and wife Carolyn, about what he had witnessed.

They all told him, "You're just acting too suspicious because you're a low-down dirty thug."

His wife Carolyn said, "You're too apprehensive about everything. You should have been a private investigator."

What she didn't know was that Mike was already involved in small-time drugs, and it was in his nature to suspect the criminal element.

He said to himself, "One day, you'll see."

The window repairman casually approached the door and rang the bell.

"Good morning," said Michael.

The repairman responded, "Good morning! I'm really sorry for the broken window! I'll fix it for you right away, sir. Oh, Mr. Banks extends his regards and really appreciates Mrs. Reid's passionate, unquestionable understanding of how unfortunate situations sometimes occur on the golf course."

Chapter 3

The next week, Mrs. Reid and the family went grocery shopping at the closest mall, thirty miles away. While they were away, Banks had no problem circumventing his way into her home with his passkey. The remote wasn't working again.

The very next month, another ball recklessly crashed through the window. But this time, Michael was definitely on it. When the repairman went into the dining room, the door was left slightly ajar. Michael's eyes popped out of their sockets, amazed at what he had witnessed. He noticed the repairman remove something from the center, just below the drawer.

"It was unbelievable! Incredible! I've never seen anything like this!" Michael whispered to himself. "To circumvent a china cabinet like this is absolutely unbelievable."

He was so astounded at what he had seen that he literally had to snap himself out of a trance. He faded into another room to avoid getting caught or appearing obviously conspicuous. When he ran into another room, the repairman thought he had heard something, so he hurried to finish, leaving in such a rush that he left a screwdriver near the light switch on the floor.

"A screwdriver on the floor? Huh! I know!" Michael thought.

At that point, Michael knew he had finally solved the mystery, though he was reluctant to tell his grandma what he had witnessed. The thought remained on the surface. Once he saw where Mr. Banks stashed his cocaine, he began plotting ways to pinch some of it without him ever knowing.

"This was Mr. Banks' personal stuff! He had pounds stored away," Michael thought.

He peeked out the window to see if the repairman had left the premises before he returned to the china cabinet to figure out how it opened. To no avail, the scope of knowledge he had was too vague to figure out the missing pieces to the puzzle. Again, he looked at the screwdriver on the floor and then discovered the cover plate on the light switch was loose. He decided, "Why not take a gamble and take off the cover plate to see what it unveils?"

In doing so, he discovered a hidden access button. He pushed it, and a sliding drawer slowly began to open. He thought he had observed drugs in the drawer but wasn't quite sure from a distance. His mind started wondering lightning fast what exactly to do. He knew for sure that he couldn't share this information with Grandma, his wife, or Sherry, but he knew he had to tell his boy Jerry.

"Michael, this is the opportunity of a lifetime for you and Jerry," he thought, "so he would think!"

"We can finally take advantage of our shortcut to success using this golden opportunity here," Michael said to Jerry.

He knew Jerry would be ecstatic to learn about the new discovery.

"Let me think! How will we distribute the stuff on this level?" Michael wondered.

Without much contemplation, he decided, "A half key per trip is transported and distributed by the ounce. That way, we avoid unnecessary trafficking and unnecessary attention."

Once he explained it to Jerry, Jerry responded, "Okay! But how about how conspicuous we'll look visiting Grandma's house too often? At some point, I assure you, it'll get very awkward for you to suddenly start coming to visit on a regular basis when everyone knows you only come around once in a blue moon."

"Jerry, you're right, man, but I can handle this. No problem."

Mike went right to Grandma and told her, "Grandma, I know in the past I must have made myself a stranger, but after spending this summer with you, I realize the importance of family. I want to make you a promise! From this point forward, I'm going to make a special effort to get here to see you once a week. You have my word, Grandma!"

Grandma replied, "Do you know how overjoyed I am to hear those words? Don't tell anybody, but you're my favorite. Everybody gets old, and everybody's going to need somebody to lean on someday! You just continue doing the right thing and stay out of trouble. That way, you'll have someone to lean on once you retire."

"Okay, Grandma!" Mike said.

Then he told Jerry, "It's on! I talked to Grandma earlier and told her how bad I felt not spending time with her, and that I was going to start coming out at least once a week to check on her in case she needs me to run errands."

It was at that moment that Mike and Jerry became extremely close—closer than they had ever imagined. They had an unbreakable commitment and were sworn to never reveal to anyone their scheme to take drugs from Mr. Banks' undisclosed compartment in the china cabinet.

Mike's heart troubled him, knowing that this drug lord hid drugs in Grandma's home without her knowledge. Allowing her to live under such critically overwhelming circumstances was awful. Young people usually thought about themselves first and others later, at least until they finally matured into adulthood. Mike was self-driven, witty, and hungry for money. His only concern was to make it through life using whatever tactic was necessary to achieve his mission.

He knew everybody needed a right-hand man, a confidant you could trust with your life and your deepest secrets never to be told or sold. That person was Jerry. Of course, his wife Carol was the runner-up, but she wasn't one of the boys. It was different.

As months advanced, Mike and Jerry constantly, week after week, conveniently stopped by to see Grandma. They would clean, cook, go to the store, and sometimes even make special meals like steak and eggs and salads served on silver platters. They were off the chart and about to take a ride they would never forget.

A month after Mike and Jerry started stealing cocaine from Banks' personal stash, it was discovered. Mr. Banks immediately changed his routine. He cunningly set up surveillance to prevent the continuation of scandalous snakes stealing from him.

"It's time to air-raid and pesticide the lawn to weed out the hidden snakes in our midst!" he decided.

He didn't know at that time whether to fault the kids, Mike and Jerry, or his staff. It was a mind-boggler, brainstorming to figure out the mystery of how someone could break the code to get into his stash unless it was someone inside the cartel or information compromised by a staff member of their lodge.

"How could someone discover how to get into the china cabinet?" Banks wondered. "I am the only one with the passkey. The only other possibility is the access switch planted inside the cover plate in Mrs. Reid's home in case of emergencies, such as a power failure or simple malfunction in the unit."

An investigation ensued. He sent Bob, a longtime buddy and private investigator, to "open the incision" and find out who was the culprit stealing his supply of cocaine. The antics continued.

Banks continued pulling stunts to get into Mrs. Reid's home. A window would accidentally break from a reckless golf ball, or a power outage would be staged to manipulate a right of passage to repair the switch. Bob would hide out in the forestry, quite a distance away, with his best friend, "Canon," who had an incredibly sharp eye, with a super lens and an instant snapshot capability that was unimaginable. Bob's job was to take pictures to figure out who was the dangerous termite or termites responsible for embarking on Banks' stash.

There were many times when Mrs. Reid and the kids would go shopping together, and Banks would delegate who would go into the home to repair the switch if, during that time, his remote to the cabinet wasn't working. Every now and then, a problem would occur. Banks desperately wanted to get to the bottom of it. He didn't want his friends finding out that someone was stealing from them.

George Wiggins was an entrepreneur, part-owner of Boatmen's Bank, a lawyer for Breckenridge, and a friend of the shareholders of the New York Stock Exchange. He also enjoyed playing his "hear no evil, see no evil" games just like his friends. His partner in crime, Mr. Banks, wasn't talking about golf. After a thorough investigation, Bob came up with nothing.

Bob reported to Banks, "I've taken numerous pictures of every descriptive detail while they were in the unit, and nothing was revealed that would suggest your staff is trying to out-hustle you in any way. Maybe we should consider other possibilities, like the kids that visit Grandma Reid."

Banks responded, "It's a ballpark, oh well; perhaps it's worth a try."

"When Jack went in to repair the window and the switch, he could have acted carelessly, and the kid Mike saw what he was doing and figured out the rest," Bob suggested, overconfidently.

Banks replied, "I'll bet that's what happened! Continue your quest, Bob. Do whatever you have to. Surely something will come up; it always does."

Mr. Banks abruptly ended the conversation, looking at his watch, realizing he had an appointment with Mr. Wiggins and Mr. Howell in one hour to discuss topics for the Ways and Means committee meeting, which would be presented to other members at the Four Seasons Hotel and Lumenier Casino.

"We need to discuss how to become better organizers and be 100 percent productive in the franchise!" he said.

"Bob, I'll get back with you when I return to get the update on our little project."

Bob Eckert replied, "Two days before your trip, I'm going to New York Manhattan, about 80 miles from here, to Mike's home at 1425 Caroline Street to see how they're living. If it's above their means, we can speculate that perhaps something's not right with that picture. But before I make that trip, I would like your permission to speak with Mrs. Reid on your behalf, to express our gratitude for the good character Mike and Jerry exhibit, and maybe spark a few things that might be hiding in the nest."

Mr. Banks said, "You have my express permission without a ceiling to do whatever you think is best."

The very next day, Bob knocked on Mrs. Reid's door.

Knock! Knock! Knock!

Mrs. Reid answered the door, "Yes, sir! Can I help you?"

"Yes! My name is Bob Eckert. Mr. Banks asked me to visit with you to acknowledge that he really admires your grandson Michael and his friend Jerry. He noticed how they come out to visit regularly and help with chores among other things. He thinks they're wonderful kids. It's not every day you see 21-year-olds looking out for Grandma."

Mrs. Reid responded, "I'm sorry, I didn't catch your name."

"Robert Eckert is my name!" Bob replied.

Mrs. Reid said, "Oh, I'm so sorry, Mr. Eckert. It's so sweet of you to say that about my grandson. I just told him the same thing three months ago, in May, when he told me that he was going to start coming out to visit me on a regular basis to take care of some of the things I may need assistance with around here."

An insidious entrapment ensued.

Bob asked, "Mrs. Reid, will you give me an address and a phone number where Mike and Jerry can be reached? There's lots of work here that needs maintenance, and it so happens Mr. Banks finds two intriguing candidates for the positions that are currently available."

Mrs. Reid, thumbing through her notepad, replied, "Oh, here it is! His name is Michael Garden, that's my grandson. His address is 1425 Caroline Street, and his phone number is 261-5521. His friend's name is Jerry Cumby. I don't have any information on him, but Michael will definitely get it for you. Oh, wait a minute! Let me look in my address book—maybe it's there. Here it is: Jerry Cumby, 1926 Carson Avenue. His home phone is 224-2121."

"Thanks, Mrs. Reid, you've really been a great help! You have a nice day!" Bob said, walking away.

Bob thought, "That was easy. Now all I have to do is take that trip to New York Manhattan to see if there's anything going on with Mike and Jerry out of the norm."

Mike and Jerry were out on the streets making connections. They had stepped their game up by a large margin; they went from selling 8 balls to ounces overnight.

"Big boys!" they thought.

Something kept telling Mike, though, that they had better slow their horses down a notch and dispense right away. With four keys tucked away, they continued to frequent the spots to drop off an ounce here and an ounce there. It was wild and enticing.

"Luckily, we didn't go down on the set," Mike said, "because we found out that two of our homeboys are getting out of prison in a few months—Dino and Do Good! These guys are notorious for selling drugs. That's all they know!"

Mike and Jerry decided on a stroke of luck to be smart and shut down their hustle, at least until Dino and Do Good got out of Rikers Island. That stalemated Mr. Banks' plan for a little while to catch the culprits stealing his product.

Mike and Jerry knew Dino and Do Good would make them rich overnight.

Jerry said to Mike, "Man, we don't have to touch nothing, just that one move from one spot to another spot!"

Mr. Eckert finally made it to Mike's home. There was a knock at the door.

Carol answered, "Who is it?"

"Mr. Eckert, an employee of Mr. Banks at Pleasure Island Resort at 1111 Willow Wood Rd., where Mike's grandmother resides."

She hurried to open the door to welcome Mr. Eckert into their home.

"What can I do for you, Mr. Eckert? What brings you this long distance?" Carol asked.

"Well, my boss, Mr. Banks, asked me to pay Mike and Jerry a visit to see if they would like the opportunity to work for Mr. Banks at Pleasure Island Resort. Will you please give Michael this number and have him give me a call to discuss his skills and possible interest in working at the resort?" Mr. Eckert said.

Carol, very excited, replied, "I most certainly will! In fact, I'll have him give you a call as soon as he gets home."

"What time do you normally expect him home?" asked Mr. Eckert.

"Well, his hours have been sporadic lately. He and Jerry have been doing odd-end jobs for a furniture company on call," Carol explained.

"Have him call me at this number: 414-217-0102," said Mr. Eckert.

"Oh!" said Carol. "I can tell you Mike and Jerry are electricians and plumbers by trade."

"Thanks, I really appreciate that information!" Mr. Eckert replied. "I'm certain it'll weigh in favorably for them with skills in that particular field."

Bob thought, "These could be our guys. They both are certified electricians and plumbers. The picture is getting more vivid as the days progress. Maybe Michael did discretely observe Jack tampering with the switch on the wall and the china cabinet. Time will tell!"

Bob was famous for his smoke screen tactics.

Later that evening, when Mike returned home, Carol told him that Mr. Eckert had been there to visit with him on behalf of Mr. Banks, the owner of the resort where his grandmother lived. Mike's mind raced.

"I wonder why!" he thought. "Man, I hope he's not accusing me of that missing cocaine."

While his mind continued to quickly race, Carol interrupted his thoughts with relief.

"Mr. Eckert was here to offer you and Jerry employment at the resort," she said.

"Wow!" he replied. "Are you serious?"

He didn't know whether to call Jerry first or Mr. Eckert.

"Did he leave you a number to call?" Mike asked.

"Yeah! Here it is!" Carol said, handing over the number.

Mike called, but there was no answer.

"I'll try calling back later," he thought. Inaudibly, talking under his breath, he added, "I'd better call Jerry and fill him in on the good news."

His phone rang about six times.

"I know he's there!" Mike muttered.

Finally, Jerry's girlfriend, Sherry, picked up the phone, gasping, seemingly out of breath, like they were in the middle of something.

She and Jerry had just finished making out on the bathroom sink. She was really mouth-watering, with dimples when she smiled, dark-skinned with a Virgin Islands complexion, pear-shaped breasts, and buttocks firmly shaped as they had never been touched—a masterpiece silhouette.

Jerry had told Mike, "My sister acts like a nymphomaniac, a man-eater!"

They both chuckled. Jerry had been dating Mike's sister since eighth grade, and their relationship was next-level unpredictable. You never knew what they would do from one minute to the next. One day, they were on an elevator, and they managed to manipulate the door so it wouldn't open. They made wild animal love on the floor, and when the elevator opened, they walked off as though nothing had happened, smiling joyfully while incomers returned the friendly greeting.

Anyway, Mike told Jerry, "Mr. Banks at Pleasure Island Resort sent one of his guys by to offer both of us a job opportunity. Isn't that crazy? We're stealing from him big time, and he offers us a job. What do you think about that, man?"

Jerry responded, "That's weird, man, but you know what? I think we should take the job because that puts us in a much better position to maneuver around the resort. Who knows? We may find the big stash. Go ahead and call him and find out what positions are open."

Mike said, "I already did, but I got no answer. I'll continue to call until I get him."

This was what they thought was their big break. Trouble was coming. They both were out searching for employment, although they were also living on the low end for supplemental income. The two of them knew they had to be employed to account for their potentially questionable income, so work was a prerequisite.

At 21 years old, Mike and Jerry really carried themselves well. They were very witty and could be very charming.

The very next day, Mike made a connection with Mr. Bob Eckert.

"Hello! My name is Michael Garden. You called yesterday!"

"Oh! Yes, Michael! I'm really excited for you guys. Mr. Banks asked me to offer the two of you employment—that's why I came by your home yesterday! We currently have janitorial jobs, electrician positions, plumbing, carpentry, driving golf carts, carrying bags, cleaning the refreshment stands, and cleaning the pool area available. We even need stable hands. Do any of those positions interest you guys?"

"Yeah, sure! Jerry and I are plumbers, electricians, and carpenters!" Mike replied.

Eckert said, "When can you come in to fill out your applications? I spoke with your grandmother about it also, and she was really excited for you and your friend Jerry. The sooner, the better."

Mike asked, "But tell me, Mr. Eckert, what is the starting salary?"

Eckert responded, "It can start as low as $7.25 or as high as $21 an hour, with incentives and an insurance benefits package included."

Mike choked, "That's great," he replied with reluctance as he attempted to clear his throat. "That's great! I'm very excited. I can't wait to fill out the application! How about the day after tomorrow, Friday, at, say, 1:00 pm?"

"Mr. Banks will have returned from his trip to St. Louis in time to make the interview scheduled here for you and Mr. Cumby," Eckert said.

"Yes, sir! We'll be here at 1:00 pm sharp!" Mike answered.

Mr. Banks and George Wiggins couldn't wait for the interview with Mike and Jerry.

Chapter 4

Four months later, Orson Blade, a.k.a. Zip, was still haunted by the horrifying memory of losing his hand. He vowed, "The pain won't ever go away until I catch that stupid punk who cut my hand off."

His boys continued to keep their ears to the ground and their eyes sharp, lurking for any sign of the creepy night crawler who had vanished like a puff of smoke into the shadows of darkness. Everybody was out trying to find the bandit's location because Zip had put a $5,000 reward on his head. There was also a $2,500 reward just for a phone call with information on where he was hiding out.

"Word better be good, though," Zip said to his boys. "I'll split you in half like a tree splitter if it's not."

Zip got a phone call. His boy picked up the phone and heard an unclear conversation about a one-armed guy with a machete at "Sawed Off's" smoking gallery, where lots of fiends hung out and smoked crack. Sawed Off was a thoroughbred turned into a lame horse—a drug addict who invited others in out of the cold to hit their stuff for a small fee—a grain, a pinch. Drug addicts were truly unpredictable. They lived in a world in which they knew none of the answers, and everything was a daredevil adventure.

Zip decided to pay a visit to see if there was any truth to the information he had received on the vine.

Sawed Off told him, "Yeah, there was a one-armed guy who stopped through, but he didn't stay long."

"Did he leave any information or a lead on where I might be able to find him?" Zip asked.

"No, man! He just said, 'It's like that!' Smoked, then disappeared seconds later. He didn't say anything to anybody, just left. He was kind of strange, though. He had this huge knife in a pouch! He pulled it out and just stared at it for a second, then put it back in its holster and started smiling with a chuckle, like he was excited about something."

Later that evening, Zip was watching the news and saw a re-run from the surveillance camera showing the one-armed Machete Bandit caught on camera. He was wearing a hooded sweater, quickly running to the car and cutting off Zip's hand. Zip fell back on the couch when he saw the video playback and put his nub to his face.

"Woo! I'm gonna kill him!" Zip said.

***

Mr. Banks walked into the hotel, and moments later, Mr. Wiggins walked in, making eye contact as they advanced toward one another to properly greet. They shook hands as they walked into the boardroom, laughing and engaging in conversation.

Mr. Howell walked through the door, interrupting, "Well, well, well, it's fancy meeting you here!"

Banks quickly responded, "Ralph, John, how is everything? How is the weather in your hometown?"

They both responded at precisely the same time, "It's an easy breeze when you got a good plan!"

A feeling obviously touched them at the same time because they were uncannily urged to turn around. Just as they did, people began crossing the threshold, and entering the meeting facility—the ballroom. Suddenly, the noise pollution increased through the excitement of seeing and chatting with really good friends who all had one vision: creating an idea that would generate financial wealth that would sustain the organization for a lifetime, and, in addition, create employment for thousands of well-deserving people in the communities at large that needed an opportunity.

These folks were high rollers nationwide—the peerless engine responsible for all strategic maneuvers used to run a phenomenally smooth operation.

"Look, Banks," said Mr. Wiggins, "Samantha, Rita, and Calvin finally made their debut. That Samantha is invigorating. She's hot!"

"Hi, ladies! Calvin!" Banks called out.

They all embraced and talked until the keynote speaker decided it was time to start the meeting. Of course, Mr. Bob Wiggins was drafted for the job; he didn't mind, as he had paid for everything—everyone's hotel room, the ballroom, and all meals while staying at the Four Seasons hotel and casino were compliments of Bob Wiggins.

Bob took the podium and greeted everyone, "Welcome, family and friends. I am delighted you all were able to make it despite your hectic daily schedules. Today, the topic for discussion is how we can increase sales in all facets of the business and, further, as a team, construct a much better incentive plan than the one we currently have in force.

"Banks and I have engaged in conversations that we think will stimulate production and growth in the industry. Exploring 'entertainment' options is a good venue to enhance sales in the franchise. It's time to put an end to partisan nonsense and get on with business. Since Trump's presidency, we've been in a slump—a decline state of mind—paralyzed to a point where we've become numb, operating on fumes with very sluggish momentum.

"We are faced with a stressed economy on all levels, and hours are being severely cut, discriminatorily stomping out healthcare benefits for all part-time employees based on policies that require a certain number of hours to qualify. Doctors, lawyers, CPAs, firemen, policemen—the list goes on and on.

"I want to acknowledge that we are in the eye of a storm that we must overcome. We must stay vigilant, yet demonstrate our elastic clause philosophy. Our flexibility will allow us to adjust to the woes that have sent even Donald Trump and the like into bankruptcy.

"An organization is only as strong as its body. Enthusiasm is its driving force and only as rich as its vision. We must strive for excellence in our business endeavors.

"What I would like for everyone to do is treat this meeting as a QA and brainstorming session that might be the key to unlocking that magical door. After that, I would like for everyone to put pen to paper and brainstorm every possible thought you may have that will:

a) Increase sales.

b) Be a better incentive plan for Pleasure Island Resorts' fifty locations.

"Once that's done, please place them in the basket with your name in case there's a perk for your incredible idea!" Bob smiled, internalizing the moment.

Hours later, Samantha, the last person to render her suggestion, committed, "Exhausted! I guess I'll go get me something to eat and a stiff..." she paused, "No, not what you think! A stiff drink to unwind! I deserve it. Would anyone care to join me?"

Banks and Wiggins accepted the invitation to discuss Banks' situation; besides, they had unfinished business.

***

Samantha was the conduit in Florida. She ran a telemarketing company filled with women who made appointments for call girls to date prominent businessmen that had players' cards from all sides of the map—global baseball players, basketball players, tennis players, politicians, you name it—even Charlie Sheen! Of course, they had a strict policy to use code "Langudo," designed by Mr. Banks, when discussing personal business to prevent breaking into the system and finding out how drug trafficking was executed, as well as prostitution, money laundering, and more.

Samantha and her telemarketing crew all had client black books with incredibly sensitive information that would compromise any of their client's futures—names, dates, and issues.

After the meeting, Mr. Banks, Mr. Wiggins, Ralph, Rita, and Samantha went out for dinner. The subject came up about someone stealing drugs from Banks' hidden compartment. To bring them up to speed, he mentioned the only two hidden places where he stashed his cocaine—the one in the wall connected to the china cabinet where he only kept twenty keys, and the one underneath the horse stable approximately eight miles from the estate.

"You guys know the inventory is 1,500 keys of cocaine," Banks said. "Lately, I've been coming up short! One third of a key missing this week, one third missing two weeks later! It doesn't stop. I know I'm not going crazy. This never happened before! I don't want you guys to think something's wrong when the money doesn't pan out, so what I've done was hire our favorite guy, Bob, to look into matters. We think we've found the culprits. We just have to be patient! In fact, call a meeting. Schedule it for the week we get back in town tomorrow. We're talking about the two young kids out of Harlem whose grandmother just moved into the resort about five months ago. We have reason to believe they stumbled upon the maintenance man repairing the controls that operate the sliding wall, which exposes the drawers in the wall connected to the china cabinet in the next unit. We have never had problems! I've always maintained an odorless chemical that distracts any machine or drug enforcement dogs from capturing the aroma that may broadcast faintly in the air. Let me ask you guys—anyone have a suggestion that may be helpful? Bob?"

Samantha responded, "What may be a good idea is to use an invisible chemical that only shows up under the light. If it turns green, that means okay; if it turns red, that's your man."

Chester replied, "Outstanding! I'm going to inform all employees that, within the next 30 days, we are going to have manufactured a temporary germ and bacteria apparatus called 'Safe Mode.' It's sophisticated and state-of-the-art, designed to prevent germs or bacteria from being imported or exported onto the estate—or perhaps a fungus while on the premises. It's for the safety of all employees, the owners, and consumers. This device is capable of reading a germ, bacteria, or fungus on a quick scan. Oh! I might add, it also has a scanner voice confirmation included that greets you by name and clocks you in. At the end of your workday, it greets you and clocks you out. This is a product that can not only be used in our establishment but in any entity—for example, fast food chains, hospitals, construction sites, law offices, just to name a few! This can be huge because it clearly demonstrates a 'healthy option for a better life.' Imagine the ability to prevent germs from entering your domain. Now, imagine being able to catch a germ or bacteria from being transported off the premises—that is huge!"

Ralph didn't say anything. He just sat and fantasized about Samantha and how he'd like to take her to his hotel room after dinner. The conversation continued for about another hour before Ralph belted out, "We're not getting anywhere with this. Why don't we just let Bob, the investigator, do his job and stay calm? That's what he gets paid for, correct?"

Chester Banks replied, "I guess you're right! Well, it's getting late. We better get out of here."

Rita quietly sat and nodded while she ate, commenting with two-liners in between the conversation.

Ralph couldn't wait to indulge in a one-on-one conversation with Samantha. Without hesitation, he asked, "Samantha, would you like to go to my hotel room and have a drink?"

Samantha replied, "Yes, I'd like that very much!"

Ralph knew from the previous engagement her drink of preference was "Cristal," so he ordered room service to bring that seductive drink that made women go crazy.

Samantha stood 5'9" with blonde hair and incredibly beautiful blue eyes, 34 years old with breasts that stood out like cherries on a tree, slender build, and a sweet voice that made you want to melt when she was in that sexy mood. She was irresistible, and Ralph was confident he wouldn't miss the opportunity he'd waited for a long time. Samantha made the move, second-guessing what was clearly exposed on the front of his forehead. She went into his restroom and came out wearing only a silk shirt—no panties—the same shirt she had worn at the dinner engagement.

"You don't waste time! I like that," said Ralph.

Samantha softly responded, "When you're in the business I'm into, you learn very quickly the vital signs that advocate sex when reading your mind. I've been contemplating this moment many nights while lying in bed thinking about you—how you make my juices flow like a soda fountain without a shut-off valve. Do you remember when you came to Florida and asked me to get you one of the girls that I thought might appease your wild, hearty appetite?"

"My boyfriend, Alex, unfortunately wandered in that day, standing right beside me. I had to accommodate you with second best because your number one girl, the one I had in mind, wasn't available, if you know what I mean." Then she smiled, turning on the song by Nicki

Minaj, "See Right Thru Me," and commenced to slowly caressing herself with wild passion.

***

The next day, Mr. Banks returned from his trip to St. Louis, Missouri, still in deep contemplation about what to do about the urgent matter. As soon as he entered the gates, he saw Mr. Eckert standing there—a moment that made him feel encouragingly content and enthusiastic about the findings learned while he was away. Bob had already assured the kids a job for the purpose of pulling everybody together under one roof, to corral or bring all elements closer to find resolve. He told Mr. Banks all he had to do was interview and hire Mike and Jerry. That way, if they were the culprits, they would know almost immediately.

"Assign them a job, and I'll take care of the rest!" Bob said.

"Okay!" Mr. Banks replied. "When should we expect these kids for the interview?"

"Today at 2:00 pm!" Bob answered.

"Good! I'll meet with you and the kids in the conference room at that time."

Chapter 5

Pulling in the gate at exactly 1:45 pm were Michael Garden and Jerry Cumby. Mike pressed the button at the gate and asked to speak with Mr. Eckert or Mr. Banks. The receptionist asked who they were and what their business was.

Mike replied, "My friend Jerry and I have a job interview with Mr. Banks and Mr. Eckert."

"Oh!" said the receptionist.

Buzz!

The gate opened.

As they slowly approached the estate with fifteen minutes before their interview, an escort and valet parker courteously greeted them, parked their car in a V.I.P. section, and escorted them to the conference room, where they were asked a series of questions before getting hired.

Banks and Wiggins thought the germ implementation couldn't have come at a better time. The current employees would think that it was just a new procedure, while Mike and Jerry would think it had been in place all the time, so they would never acquire suspicion when putting their hands under the light at the end of each workday—not realizing that if your hand turned blue, you were not the snake, but if it turned yellow, it meant you stole the cocaine.

The software installed was very sophisticated! It acknowledged who a person was by touch and, through AI intelligence, computed color code information to reveal who had stolen the drugs. Each key of cocaine had an invisible liquid that showed up only under specific light. Only four people were allowed to handle the goods if their hands showed up yellow: Banks, Howell, the jock, John, and Kelly, his good friend. Kelly was a wild panther, woven in with many other cougars and panthers responsible for managing the telemarketing enterprise in Florida with Samantha.

She also resided at Pleasure Island Resort and responsibly managed her business via the internet. They were the only ones permitted to handle the bags after delivery. Everyone else with clandestine involvement in the enterprise only made contact when picking up packages for delivery from John or the jock. Banks, Wiggins, and their boys didn't need shark repellent—they were the sharks, devouring anyone who crossed the cartel like piranhas, spitting out bones for the dogs to finish.

Banks and Bob had hired Mike and Jerry for general contracting work at the resort. They were handymen who took care of the pool, golf course, electrical work, and plumbing jobs, sometimes even working the horse stable. The two of them were thrilled to learn they had gotten jobs working for Mr. Banks! They couldn't wait to get to Grandma's house to share the good news. The very second Mike rang the bell, the door opened as if Grandma had been watching him and Jerry walk up to the front door.

Suddenly, a news flash interrupted the TV program—the red-light machete bandit had struck again, but this time it was a near miss. Cortez, also known as "Tez," described the moment while waiting at the red light. "This guy came up from behind. I didn't see him at first," he said. "It wasn't until a bee flew into my car, landing on the steering wheel, that I moved my hand to fan it away. Then, I heard this loud boom." He turned to see a man with a beard pulling a gruesome-looking knife out of the door.

He managed to get clear and immediately called the police department. The officer knew Cortez from the neighborhood as a small-time drug dealer who liked everyone to think he was the man because he always dressed well.

Officer Simmons found it strangely amusing. He thought Cortez might struggle to traffic drugs if he lost a hand. Snapping out of the thought, he began questioning Cortez about the assailant. "Can you recall what he looked like, what type of clothing he was wearing, or anything distinguishing like tattoos?"

Cortez replied, "He ran so quickly, I didn't get a good look. I only managed to catch a side view, but I did notice he wore a beard."

Cortez didn't see it as breaking any code to give information on this guy. He felt the bandit was disgracing the game. "What's his motivation?" he wondered. "The guy's a nut, popped out of a shell and thrown in the trash. How did he pull that off?"

No one knew the bandit parked his car a few blocks from each scene to prevent anyone from seeing what he drove daily. Plus, he had a false arm that he never wore. I got to tell you, it seemed like he was losing his touch because he never missed, and this carelessness caused him to sprain an ankle. That's an injury hard to fully recover from in a short time. He knew after that blunder he had to take some time off because he realized he couldn't maneuver swiftly enough to get away.

Before the news could hit the press, the special unit was on it. The investigators had requested teletypes, a sketch artist, psychologist, fingerprint, and DNA experts; Operation "Shut Down" took it personally because one of their own had lost a limb to this sadistic maniac! The chief really put together a good team! The very second the rubber hit the pavement, they worked diligently 24/7 around the clock. Chief Hightower was famous for his honorary award that commended his stance against unstoppable odds; he was determined to make the police department better by going into the "No Zone," where all the police departments' hidden secrets were kept. Once in the vault, it never came out! Those secrets included disgraceful malpractice stories that would break the bank; for instance, police officers engaging in discriminatory issues, plagiarism, racial profiling, misrepresentation of their department, broken chain of custody, throwdowns, and more. Hightower was an advocate of the phenomenal case law cited in *Miller versus Whaley* 581 S.W.2d 9: "False reporting shall not be tolerated, nor shall failure to report."

His plan to bring an end to this insane corruption would take an unprecedented, brilliant plan, so he instituted a new policy that read, "All police officers are required to rotate partners every ninety days." That way, two officers couldn't become extremely close to a point of corruption.

When two officers served together perpetually, they took on a friendship, and through this friendship, statistics showed allegations of police misconduct had a tendency to occur; every day, they were confronted with unimaginable, provocative opportunities to withhold evidence from the department, money, drugs, and "throwdowns"—a gun placed at the scene when the police killed somebody unjustifiably. He also thought about what the opposition might say to keep their partners together as long as they were in the department! "When you work with an officer, you create a pact with one another to always have each other's back." News flash—all officers are professionals and also qualify to have your back. When this new policy came out on memorandum, the department was uneasy at first, but they adjusted. Chief Hightower was about to make history. Since before J. Edgar Hoover and Prohibition, police officers were paired up for their entire stay at the department unless they decided a change would be advantageous for the theme.

The same concept was used in big franchises today, like rental car services such as Avis, Budget, or Enterprise. Once a manager was there for a year, they transferred to another location. In theory, that prevented them from getting too close to other managers who might have insidious notions to circumvent or compromise sales for personal gain.

The goal of Operation Shut Down was to find out whether there was any conduit between the victims, whether there was some type of relationship. Reports conclusively showed all the victims had something in common.

They all had a criminal history and played on the same playground—cocaine and heroin! The machete bandit once went to Rock Um's pad to pick up a package of cocaine, and Rock Um couldn't help mentioning, "Man, I saw the news. How you be ripping arms off people! Man, you be hurting the game, 'G.' Them brothers are gangsters! Man, you must be insane. I like it, though, 'cause I got beef with all them butchers."

The red-light machete bandit replied, "I'm not insane, player; they're the ones who are insane because they allowed me to sneak up on the blind side! Man! They know it's like that! You know there's no love; cut my arm off! This—it is deep with me, son!"

Banks went to his office as Mike and Jerry exited the conference room area to catch up on his mail and messages while he was away in St. Louis. Thumbing through his mail, he noticed without reading that a shipment was scheduled. He knew at a glance because it was a personal message written in code. Anything written in code obviously meant a member of the cartel sent it.

Bruno sent a message:

1 2 2 1 3 3 2

1__ /1 1/ /1 1__[___ /3 [___ [___ ___ [ ]] 1/] 2/ ___]] __ [___

2 1 2 1 2 3 1 3 3 1

1 3 1 4

] [___] /3] ___ ___...

3 3 1

"A cocaine shipment is to arrive Thursday." Banks responded to the message: "Those Colombian boys don't play with the quality of their cane. They've got the best stuff circulating in this town. It smells like milk and eggs in a supermarket; as soon as it hits the shelves, it's gone—like 'Gone with the Wind's' Clark Gable!"

That discrete language had saved their lives too many times; it wasn't often you saw it lying around for anyone to read, but there was always the chance someone might slip and forget to tuck it away with the hectic schedules and events facilitated daily. Mike asked Jerry, "Man, did you see that hot receptionist who might be Mr. Banks' daughter? I think she's got a thing for me! I know that look when I see it!"

Jerry replied, "Time will tell! We're in now! She's fine, with that sexy dress clinging to her well-sculpted body that looks like a perfect work of art; God had to clock in overtime to manifest that."

Mike responded, "Man, I can't believe he said we start tomorrow morning at 7:00 a.m. When he said that, we both responded at the same time, 'We won't let you down, you'll see.'" The very next day, Mike and Jerry arrived ready to work. Oddly enough, Jack Hornsby greeted them as their supervisor.

"Hi! My name is Mr. Hornsby. I assume you are Michael and Jerry?"

"You're right!" said Jerry.

"What I would like you gentlemen to do is take that wheelbarrow by the garage, fill it with these fine rocks, and fill the holes on the jogging trail. Mr. Banks jogs every morning thirty minutes after breakfast! As you can see, the rain has washed the rocks down onto the road. When you're finished there, go to the refreshment stands at the golf course and clean the restroom; you'll find the cleaning supplies in the closet to the right. Call me on your radio when those assignments are complete."

Mike told Jerry, "I hope it gets easier! They have us working crazy hours."

Jerry replied, "Man, it doesn't matter! We've got the best benefits in town—health care, sick leave with pay, vacation pay, and a dip in his cocaine every chance we get."

They both smiled, thinking that someday they'd own properties from coast to coast. The first day wasn't half bad. Mike made it home by 4:30 p.m., and Carol didn't get home until 6:00 p.m., working 9 to 5 as a physical therapist making eight dollars an hour. Mike's sister Sherry worked as a supervisor over the cleaning crew at the Holiday Inn, ensuring rooms were cleaned as people checked out. At six o'clock, Mike heard the key in the door—it was Carol.

"Hi, baby!" he said. "How was your day?"

"It was good," she replied, "pushing and pulling patients all day. Other than that, just another day on the job! How was your day?"

"I had a really rough day, but it worked out well."

"Come here," Carol said as she slowly unbuttoned her top. Mike kissed her neck as her clothes fell to the floor. Carol was young and innocent to the streets, but that 21-year-old certainly wasn't a stranger to the sheets. Her shapely body spelled *swaggalicious*—her erect nipples like ripe grapes. Her toned stomach made Mike's mouth water, leading him to her midsection, where a pierced stomach ring dangled provocatively. As they fell onto the bed, her thighs parted, welcoming him. The minute he touched those walls, he exploded... but got right back in the saddle and rode for a while.

Afterward, they showered together, playing around like kids in a bubble bath. Mike got a bit serious and said, "Carol, now that I have a real job, here's what we're going to do: We'll establish good credit, and Jerry and Sherry will do the same. Once we reinvent ourselves as a team, we'll borrow money to rehab homes, selling and renting them out. The equity will grow, and we'll use it to keep building. Every so often, we'll sell one property to pay off two that we got at auction. When we hit thirty properties, we'll borrow the big bucks."

Mike added, "We can do it because we've got skills and audacity. We're carpenters, plumbers, and electricians. What more do we need to succeed, other than good management skills?"

Carol replied, "It sounds like an excellent idea, as long as you don't get sidetracked again."

Chapter 6

The next month, they heard that Dino and Do Good had gotten an early release from Rikers Island due to overcrowding. They went in for robbing Little John's pizza joint, but drugs were in their blood; their whole generation smoked, shot, and sold from the projects to the suburbs. They drank, ate, and slept with drugs on their minds, still dressing well, flaunting their swag, and hanging out at elite clubs—their favorite spot being the Flamingo, the hottest spot in town. Mike and Jerry knew exactly where to find them and decided to head to the Flamingo, where it was comedy night and casual attire.

Mike, Carol, Jerry, and Sherry arrived early to get good seats, the girls having no idea of the real reason they were there. An hour later, Mike spotted Gary and Harvey Henson, a.k.a. Dino and Do Good.

"This is where the roller coaster ride begins," Mike whispered to Jerry, "and we forgot to strap on our seat belts."

Mike nudged Jerry, motioning to follow him. Turning to Carol and Sherry, he said, "Would you ladies excuse us? We're going to the restroom." The girls nodded as they approached Dino and Do Good at the bar, who stood watching the crowd while enjoying their first drink in five years. Dino noticed them first, nudging Do Good, "Look who's coming this way!"

"What's going on?" Jerry asked. "I heard you just got out! What are your plans?"

Dino replied, "Man, you know we're down like that!"

Mike interrupted, "Looking for work?"

Do Good responded quickly, "Yeah! You got some for us?"

Mike replied, "I've got to tell you, it's really good, good! We've been waiting impatiently for you to come home. We've got a pretty good supply now, with access to more, but we needed someone to help us turn it over. We know you guys know exactly where to dump it."

Dino asked, "When can we check this good stuff out?"

"Well," Mike replied, "Jerry and I have work tomorrow, but we can still meet at the old hangout. You remember Little Johnnie, don't you?"

"Yeah, man!" they both replied.

"Meet us at his place at six o'clock."

"It's a deal!" Dino said. "We'll see you there; don't be late."

The next day, they met them with two ounces of cocaine, just to see how fast they could move the product. They knew Dino and Do Good had just come home, but they also knew these two knew every crack in the pavement and the streets, as well as a surgeon, knew smoking caused cancer.

Two days later, Mike got a phone call from Dino.

"Man, we're finished with that snack you gave us. Can we get up?"

"Sure," said Mike. "Meet us at the same spot, same time today."

This time, they upped the ante and gave them twice the amount to see how fast they could move a quarter key rocked up. Dino and Do Good paid them $3,000 out of the $4,000 they made from cracking up two ounces of cocaine. Mike and Jerry looked at each other with a smile of victory.

"Man, I think we've got it made," Jerry said to Mike, "as long as Dino and his brother don't get clumsy and fumble the ball."

Chapter 7

That arrangement went on for months without problems, thank God. When the calendar year turned over, Dino and Do Good were turning over kilos in a matter of days. Things were really looking up!

Personas changed, dress codes changed, hangouts changed, business concepts changed—everything suddenly changed. Mr. Eckert was getting dismayed because nothing had turned up. "Could it be that your boys are miscalculating the shipment order?" he asked.

"I don't think so," said Bob. "I know quite a bit has come up missing, but maybe they think we're onto them and they've stopped for a while." Bob was reading Mike and Jerry just right and didn't know it.

"What do you say I take some time off to spend with my wife and kids? Lately, she's been on me for spending crazy hours here, trying to get to the root of our troubles."

"You're right, Bob," said Mr. Banks. "It's been rough, and you deserve time off with your family. Plus, there haven't been any recent attempts. Go ahead and enjoy yourself; take two weeks off unless I call you with an emergency."

"Oh, and here are plane tickets to Orlando, Florida, for you and your family to stay at the Renaissance Hotel. How's that?"

"Thanks, Banks! My wife is going to be completely swept off her feet when she hears the news. Thanks a million!"

Banks replied, "Ah, don't mention it. Be sure to tell Samantha and the ladies at the telemarketing agency I send my love."

Two days into Mr. Eckert's trip to Florida, Mike and Jerry decided to strike again. Dino and Do Good had come home, and the product was moving tremendously fast. He had kept his promise to Grandma, so it wasn't unusual for him and Jerry to pop up, especially since they both worked for the resort. Coincidentally, Mr. Banks' guard was down; he had just sent Bob on vacation.

The two youngsters slipped in and stole a key from the cabinet; gloves were their best friends, allowing them to circumvent the scanner daily, both before and after work. Banks didn't realize anything was missing until the next week's inventory. Furious to find that the "snake" had returned, he was also strangely delighted, seeing it as another chance to catch the thieves. He thought of them as "thieves" because they always navigated in pairs; misery loves company.

Banks, thinking about his situation, picked up the phone and began dialing the Florida area code with Bob in mind, but for some strange reason, he got sidetracked and called Samantha. She was in her office, as usual, managing the business, and he admired her ability to make things happen on the east coast.

Since he'd made the call, he decided to update her. "The idea to use that machine to find out who's stealing was a good one," he said. "It would be an ingenious idea to use the same technology in all fast-food restaurants!"

"Well," said Samantha, "I'm sure you had the patent attorney execute that plan expeditiously."

"You're right!" Banks replied. "Let me ask, though, how are the girls doing? Have there been any infractions lately?"

Samantha thought for a moment. "We have this one girl, Michelle, who's been having problems with her boyfriend's insecurities and a few other minor issues. Sometimes those personality clashes get on my nerves, but other than that, everything's fine in sunny Orlando, Florida. Business is getting better! We get new prospects all the time—some good, others, well... throwbacks. You know the business."

Samantha's telecommunication service was located downtown, in a spacious room with sixty cubicles for her employees. There were fifty women and two men who knew how to "speak in tongues." Their market was life insurance policies, special hair products, and a guaranteed floor stripper called "No Huff No Puff, Just Wipe Away." Behind all that mascara were 30 of the most gorgeous, intellectual, highly energized, and ambitious exhibitionists with no ceiling. They were off the charts! These women would walk a tightrope from the tallest building in Manhattan in a 60-degree wind chill!

I have to tell you, these girls were a phenomenal work of art, eager to please with the juiciest "Florida peaches" in the state, enough to make your mouth tingle! The girls rarely had problems with their dates because they had a phenomenal screening team that observed each candidate through a two-way glass. The team included Sanders, a former police officer hired with fringe benefits; Lawanda Sharp, a.k.a. "Brown Sugar," a former prostitute turned fashion entrepreneur; Catherine Steel, the company's representative and consultant; April Williams, a sociologist; and Joan Spears, a psychologist. Together, they determined good or bad candidates for the girls.

All the girls were part of the company to do legitimate work and sometimes make clandestine appointments for clients after hours. They could go if they had to, especially for a big spender. It was always a busy day at the office. Samantha's phone rang.

"Banks, can you hold for just a second, please? I have a call on the other line."

"Sure," Banks replied.

"Samantha!" said Beth on the other line. "Ms. Linda Mac is here to see you."

"Thank you, Beth! Send her in."

Instantly, a short, gorgeous lady walked through the door with ridiculous confidence.

"Yes, Ms. Samantha?"

"I have a client who just arrived at the Holiday Inn. He's in room 222. His name is Sir Charles Sterling—a nicely built gentleman weighing about 205 pounds. I need you to take care of him for me."

Linda replied, "I'm on my way…"

Samantha called Beth back and told her to send Barbara into her office. Barbara, a tall black Amazon, strutted like the queen of the cats, walking with tastefully enticing attributes that made everyone stare in awe. Her body defined the word "entrapment."

"Barbara, I just got a call—a long-time customer is in town! You've met him before. He requested you specifically. He has a new girlfriend who goes both ways and would like you to be that special third partner."

Barbara replied, "Let me guess! Harry Summerville?"

"You're right!" Samantha confirmed. "Meet him at his condo at 1124 Ocean Shore Drive at 1 p.m. He'll be delighted to know you're available for his private party."

Barbara walked toward the door, thanking Samantha. Before she could leave, Samantha called the receptionist to send in Tina Lopez, Monica Smith, and Michele Crenshaw to her office. Beth paged them over the intercom to report to Samantha's office. Entering the room together, Monica asked on behalf of everyone, "What's going on, Samantha?"

"Ladies," Samantha replied, "Rev. Mitchell's cousin is getting married, and he's arranging a bachelor's party through a close friend. He doesn't want anyone to know he's associated with this godforsaken party, but we know better. He'll make an appearance somehow—he loves young, fine women, and the three of you are extremely attractive in all aspects."

At that moment, Ralph Wiggins rang the line. Beth picked up, asking how she could help.

"This is Ralph Wiggins, and I'd like to speak with Ms. Samantha Willis," he said.

"Can you hold for just a second while I connect you?" Beth replied. Then, she paged Samantha, "You have a call on line 6. It's Mr. Ralph Wiggins."

Samantha quickly transferred to speak with him, excited. "Hello, Ralph! How are you? I was just thinking about our rendezvous in St. Louis. I really enjoyed experiencing the true essence of a man who can be loving and tender, getting emotionally charged in the moment instead of just taking me for a ride."

Wiggins replied, "Maybe one day soon we can pick up where we left off because we're still in play mode."

Samantha responded, "That sounds like a plan! Let me check my calendar before making future plans. Business has been demanding these last few months, and it's hard to opt out right now with new client orientation and a boost in consumer enrollment. Let me get back to you next week after I clear some of these appointments."

"I'll look forward to your call!" Wiggins said.

Samantha hung up from Ralph and called Beth to send in Monica, a.k.a. "Cream Delight." Monica was totally irresistible, like a cheetah always rising to the top like cream. Her clients admired her like she was a sapphire. She could twist her body in unimaginable ways, like a contortionist using choreographic tricks as foreplay, making her clients want to savor every moment. She was the highest-paid in the business.

Meanwhile, Banks was going crazy. He wanted to hire an investigator to investigate his investigators because he had a flashback, realizing he hadn't done inventory before Bob left for vacation. He was at his wits' end, unable to crack the culprits' plan. Banks thought Bob and his wife were out partying in Florida, snorting up his cocaine, and wondered if that's why Bob wanted the vacation. Not trusting any investigator for the job, he called a dear childhood friend, Donald Howell, a member of the organization since birth.

Banks told Donald, "I'm still dealing with my dilemma. The same problem keeps happening—keys of cocaine disappear right under my nose! I'm beginning to suspect my own guy, Bob, who's been my P.I. since we started this operation!"

Donald replied, "Sorry, but I can't assist you personally. However, I recommend the best in the business—Starlet Templeton. She's savvy, knows exactly how to accomplish her objective, and is incredibly charming and tenacious. If the price is right, she'll do whatever it takes. The sky's the limit. She's my lady luck."

Banks, Wiggins, and Donald each had personal clients who came to the resort to pick up ounces of cocaine for personal use. This clientele was "off the chain," including news broadcasters, writers for the *Post Dispatch*, doctors (who you'd think could prescribe their own drugs but not cocaine), and lawyers who enjoyed the euphoria as they walked into court and stayed awake all night preparing for trials. One jeweler with a huge cocaine appetite sold jewelry to stars like Jennifer Lopez, Jay-Z, Beyoncé, and P. Diddy. The list went on, with movie stars, country singers, R&B artists, and rappers. All other drug distribution was handled by dealers for the cartel, discretely planted in homes across neighborhoods, dropping keys like rain in monsoon season. Banks and his boys stayed humble during peaceful times, but when someone screwed up, sparks flew like a man standing in water holding an electric wire.

Dino and Do Good's parole officers and the police department were on high alert, prowling around their business. They had been snooping for months since the pair came home. Six keys of cocaine had slipped through Dino and Do Good's fingers like Michael Jordan with a basketball. They both owned black '07 BMWs with smoke-gray leather interiors. Their vice was dice, always rolling and saying, "What they hit for?" They dressed in expensive diamond rings, ridiculous chains, Rolex watches, Armani suits, and Perry Ellis. But hanging out at the club didn't help matters; it wasn't a good look.

It so happened that the police department had assigned undercover officers to follow Dino and Do Good and placed "painters" on the streets—a term for informants, who "paint pictures" with their information.

Two officers, Jennifer Kelly and Travis McCray, were undercover at the Flamingo Club, presenting themselves as a couple. Travis went to the restroom upon entering the club, while Jennifer wandered over to the bar to strike up a conversation.

"Sweetie, let me get you a drink?" Do Good asked.

"I don't think that's a good idea," she replied, "because my fiancé might get a little jealous. Here he comes now!"

Travis walked over, asking, "Honey, what did you want to drink?"

"Millers," she replied with a smile.

Travis continued the conversation, giving the impression that he and Jennifer were boosters who stole clothes and jewelry, knowing most young players in the game prided themselves on their swag—clothes and jewelry meant everything.

Dino barged into the conversation. "Hey, playa, did you say you knock off all the famous name-brand clothes and jewelry? Man, you're the kind of playa we need to hook up with because we get our grind on big-time."

Jennifer responded, "What's your definition of big-time? You might be another one of those brothers who talks a good game, but when it's time to deliver the goods, you're nowhere to be found."

"Girlfriend, we're one hundred! We just dropped six keys in one week."

Travis said, "Give us a number where you can be reached." They exchanged numbers, and Jennifer and Travis hung around for about thirty more minutes before leaving.

Mike and Jerry were very low-key in their business. They each had two hundred and fifty thousand dollars stashed. "Do Good" and Dino had sixty thousand each tucked away because their recreational pastimes—clothes, jewelry, gambling, and snorting—devoured most of their earnings. Sometimes, I wonder why addicts dodge bullets to stay alive, only to act like they want to commit suicide, heading straight to the dope house to buy lethal drugs that could take their lives as easily as the bullets they struggle to avoid. I guess that's why education is so important; without it, life is like a ship without a sail, waiting for a strong wind.

Chapter 8

The following week, the two of them were riding together in Do Good's car. He had been drinking Patron, smoking Kush, and wasn't paying attention to the road while talking on his cell phone. Suddenly, the police noticed the car weaving and decided to pull them over for a possible traffic citation. When the officers approached the car, they asked the driver to roll down the window. As soon as he hit the button, a peculiar, funky odor filled the air, hitting the officer's face, which gave him probable cause to search the vehicle.

Before searching, the officer told the driver, "The reason for the stop is that you were exceeding the speed limit by twenty miles an hour."

Dino should have kept his mouth shut, but he blurted out, "My brother wasn't speeding! I was looking at his speedometer right before you turned your lights on us. Sir, would you care to see what it reads?"

"No, that won't be necessary," said the officer's partner. "Let's search these guys and see if they have drugs."

Officer Kelly pulled ten grams out of Dino's pocket and found a loaded handgun underneath Do Good's seat. The two brothers were immediately taken to county jail. They couldn't post bail, not because they were recidivists frequently in and out of the system, but because they were parole violators, who are typically held until a parole officer decides whether to detain or release them, based on the nature of the offense.

Dino and Do Good were still breathing a sigh of relief, thinking back to just having dropped off five ounces of cocaine and SKS assault rifles before getting stopped. Now, they were heading back to prison for five years after only one year of freedom. Mike and Jerry knew the brothers had gotten caught but didn't think the courts would send them back to prison so quickly. They weren't too disappointed, though, because things had been moving at an incredibly fast pace, and if it continued, the bottom was destined to fall out. Mike and Jerry were making money so fast they'd nearly forgotten about their original real estate plan.

A week later, the brothers were sent back to Rikers. Mike got a call from Dino explaining what happened. "The courts sent us back on the parole violation while they wait to decide if there'll be a trial on the drug and gun charges. As soon as we're out, I'll look you up."

Mike replied, "Well, man, if you need anything, don't hesitate to call."

No one ever found out who their source was because it all happened so suddenly. Officers Jennifer and Travis had to call off their drug investigation. Unfortunately, they were off-duty when the arrests happened and couldn't intervene to prevent the brothers' release.

Meanwhile, Mike and Jerry, moving right along with their plan, went out and purchased a four-bedroom home, which they converted into a five-bedroom with a walkout patio deck connected to the master bedroom. The equity skyrocketed. They had paid thirty grand for the home at auction, and it was initially appraised at one hundred thousand. Now, it was worth one hundred and fifty thousand. Taking a chance, they went to Mr. Banks.

"Mr. Banks," Mike began, "we bought a four-bedroom home, fixed it up, and now it's worth 150 thousand. We only paid thirty for it. Cutting to the chase, we'd like to borrow fifty thousand from you or get a loan at your bank. All you need to do is vouch for our credibility as hard-working young guys who just haven't had a chance to establish credit. We'll use the house as collateral."

Banks responded, "I'll tell you what, guys. I'll refer you to a friend with high recommendations. I'm sure he can help you out. Let me call him and make the arrangements, and I'll get back to you tomorrow. How does that sound?"

"That sounds great!" they both replied simultaneously.

After Banks hung up, Jerry did a victory gesture, pulling both hands down, saying, "That sounds like a winner!" This gave them the long-awaited opportunity to wash one hundred and forty thousand dollars squeaky clean. They were finally on their way to a comfortable lifestyle. They considered trading in their cars for new ones but quickly thought that wouldn't be smart; they didn't want the bank to think they had too much outstanding debt.

Reflecting on Mike and Jerry's big move, Banks thought, *They've only been with me for a year. With other expenses, how could they come up with that much money in such a short time?*

The next day, Banks called and told them they had an appointment with Mr. Ralph Wiggins, co-owner of Boatman/Mercantile Bank. His office was located in downtown Manhattan on Broadway, and their appointment was scheduled for 10:00 a.m.

Jerry asked Mike, "Should we ask about work schedules for tomorrow?"

Banks overheard and replied, "Just consider it a paid vacation day. I admire your overzealous motivation. It's refreshing to see young people strive forward. I wish you both the best."

"You're a mentor and a friend," Mike replied. "You've helped us in so many ways, you'll never know."

Banks smiled. "I'm proud to be an inspiration. Thank you."

The appointment with Mr. Wiggins was a success. Banks already knew, having personally told Ralph to extend them the loan. With the money, they bought five houses.

They continued to work for Banks, but as soon as they could get off the clock, they would rush home to grab a bite to eat, change clothes, and head right back out the door, carrying tool bags and other tools small enough to fit in the trunks of their two cars. They went straight to the property chosen to be the first to repair, discussing the possibility of taking short vacations at the resort periodically to complete each project until all were done.

"It so happens vacation time is available now; it's been a year since we were hired. Let's put in for that time off and hopefully get lucky with the same days off. Maybe Mr. Banks will understand our objectives!"

"Plus, I haven't spent any downtime with my girl, and neither have you. We deserve this time off." Changing the narrative, Jerry said to Mike, "We can sell the first home we finish for 80 thousand, pay off the loan with Mr. Wiggins, and use the extra 30 to rehabilitate two more properties. Once the equity is there, we can go back to Wiggins without using Banks to get us in. We're already in! Borrow a hundred thousand and keep rolling."

While Mike and Jerry were on vacation, a big truck pulled into the resort, heading toward the horse stable, about a football field's length from the front gate. Banks met with Cortez and Martinez, the two jocks who knew about the drug stash under the horse stable. In the horse stall was a trapdoor covered with a mix of straw, dirt, and horse manure. This trapdoor led to a tunnel 20 feet down and extending approximately one block, with enough space to install tracks to navigate on a trolley car system. There was one other way out that no one knew of except Banks and the designers. He kept an untamed horse named Stub, short for "Stubborn," in the stall with the trapdoor. Stub only respected two people: Cortez and Banks. Anyone else who entered the stall risked getting attacked by Stub; he was as wild as an "Indian on Boone's Farm!"

Starlet, the investigator, had been working on the estate for quite some time. Though she was initially hired to investigate the missing cocaine, Banks had also hired her as his personal bookkeeper and consultant. Seeing Starlet walking toward the stable, Banks hurried to intercept her, definitely not wanting her to see what was happening.

"Hi, Starlet!" said Banks.

She smiled. "Hi! I just came up here to tell you our situation is just like taking a car to the shop. You hear certain noises, but when you get it to the shop, it no longer makes the noise."

They were interrupted by the truck driver, "We're all done! I'll see you next time." Starlet didn't know that 1,500 keys of cocaine had just been dropped off. This pipeline connection took place every week.

About 80 miles away in New York, the Red Light Machete Bandit, his girlfriend, and their partner Larry walked through the door to his apartment, yelling, "I got first," indicating he was the first to use the syringe. They'd just scored a package of heroin from Young Blood. It could be stepped on six times; it was potent enough to kill a horse! The Bandit got the syringe and a grease top, cooked it up, drew his usual amount, and injected it into his arm. Larry asked, "How was it?" and all he could say was, "This s—t is good as a motha!" He passed out. He'd met his match; the stuff was too potent. No accolades for that—he passed out instantly. His girlfriend and Larry didn't know what to do.

They both panicked, not knowing what to do. Larry thought quickly, "Carla, get some ice, a towel, a glass of milk, and some salt." She frantically raced through the house, gathering everything he asked for. Larry had heard all the stories about what to do in situations like this but had never had to apply them. He had no other choice now, so he tried "dope fiend surgery" as suggested by other addicts. First, he mixed the salt and water together in the same grease top until the salt had dissolved completely. Then he injected the salty water into the Bandit's vein, force-fed him the milk while he lay unconscious, and last, applied ice in a towel to his private area. Sometimes it worked! It didn't work here, though. Larry could have killed his friend. Addicts never asked one another whether they had high blood pressure or diabetes—salt could have been the worst enemy for someone with high blood pressure.

Panic set in. Larry decided to stop everything and get him to the hospital, but he couldn't carry him across the threshold because he was wanted. Larry drove him to the hospital and managed to get a wheelchair. They struggled to get him into the chair, and Carla rolled him right through the doors. They asked her what happened. She replied, "He overdosed on heroin." They quickly rushed him into the OR to be pumped. The nurse asked Carla to join her to register her boyfriend. She knew giving his real name was a definite no, so she gave the nurse an alias name and address, providing no other information.

When the Red Light Machete Bandit finally came around in the hospital, he got out of bed and walked out. As he exited down the stairwell, a lady noticed his missing arm and called the police, saying she thought she'd just seen the Red Light Machete Bandit. The special task force arrived within minutes. In their questioning, they asked what he looked like and what he was wearing. She said, "I called because it looked very suspicious seeing a patient walk completely off the hospital premises in a gown."

Officer Henderson interrupted, telling his partner, "I'm going to check with registration to see if a one-armed patient came in within the past few days to see if we can get some DNA."

Henderson approached the desk and asked if they had registered a one-armed patient within the last three days, and the lady at the desk replied, "Can you excuse me for a second while I ask other staff?" The registration personnel in the next cubicle overheard the conversation and remembered the man being wheeled in, unconscious, by a woman.

"What was the circumstance?" the officer asked. "Was there any DNA sample drawn from this individual?"

"Of course," she replied. "Let me get someone who can better assist you with that." She called the physician assigned to his case. Walking through the automatic doors was Doctor Jonathan McCall. The nurse acknowledged Officer Henderson, introducing him to Doctor McCall. Henderson explained to the doctor the story about the Red Light Machete Bandit, and the doctor said he saw that on the news. He went further to ask him, "Did you secure DNA on the patient?" and he responded, "Yes, but it would take at least a day to retrieve that report." Henderson told him, "That's fine! Here's my card! Give me a call as soon as that information comes across your desk." "Sure thing," he said.

Chapter 9

The next day, Henderson got a phone call from the hospital. The doctor gave him Eugene Adams' name, social security number, and a former address used over two years ago. Now they had ID on a possible suspect! Henderson's team scrambling hastily; they now has a lead on a man with one arm who might be the perpetrator. They caught up with Eugene Phillips at his mother's house, sitting at the kitchen table eating dinner; that wasn't where he lives! He was just visiting, and the police luckily showed up minutes later. They took him to the station for questioning and put him on a tainted lineup. He was the only person on the lineup with one arm! Talk about pointing the finger right down somebody's throat without just cause! The department was desperate to charge somebody. The entire state was terrorized by this anonymous maniac who might strike at any time!

Eugene walks out of the police department. Outfoxed again! You can't identify a person as a suspect purely on the fact he has a missing arm; there are thousands of people with an arm missing! Their plan failed this time…thanks to rotating police officers!

Back in Florida, Rev. Mitchell's party was all set to go. Cedric gets married one week from today, and tonight is his bachelor's party. The reverend's curiosity was bubbling! He had to come up with a really good reason to show up at the party considering pastors don't indulge in those sorts of things. He arrived much later than the rest of the guys; he knocked on the door, and without asking who it was, the door opened. Pete's eyes popped out of his head, and his bottom jaw totally clasped. The Bishop told Pete to relax, "There's nothing wrong with the Bishop stopping in at the party to have a non-alcoholic beverage toast with my little cousin. I'm not gonna stay because I have a previous engagement with my accountant." Once the Bishop made his presence known, the tone changed on a dime. Robert, whispering in Randy's ear, "Let's spike the Bishop's drink!" He'll never know the difference…"

They had two big tubs, one filled with non-alcoholic and the other gin and juice. Robert asked the Bishop, "Would you like a non-alcoholic drink?" "Yeah! Sure! That'll be great!" So they put very little tangerine and orange juice in his drink. He knew they had spiked his drink but just pretended he couldn't distinguish any difference. That was his opportunity to act in a manner unbecoming a man of the cloth; he wanted to touch and play with the young girls Samantha sent to the party. He had an appetite he couldn't fulfill that night because he would only embarrass himself. The freak could have eaten all the peaches in the room without coming up for air one time; women in G-strings and topless all over the place! That was too intense for Bishop…After a while, he got warm! He had forgotten he told them that he only wanted to toast the groom and leave. As he fumbled to loosen his shirt to get comfortable, a young lady about 26 years old walked over and said, "Please allow me." The Rev. was in awe! He hoped no one saw what was going on, but that was the drink talking at that point. She momentarily walked away from the Bishop and started toward the groom, rubbing her tits in his face, then laid on the floor and spread her legs wide, exposing the goods. She got up and bent over to shake her behind provocatively; everyone in the room was hot and bothered after that show, especially the Rev. One young lady named Sharon recognized him right away, and he hushed her very quickly with his eye contact so the others wouldn't find out about his scandalous endeavors.

No one could just walk in and ask Samantha to send girls to a party unless she had some history with that person; the Bishop was a regular customer who has been straddling the fence since Genesis! He wasn't hot, warm, or lukewarm; he was a con artist with a silk tongue who spent time in prison learning the word while going through his foxhole prayers to convince the prison administration that he had turned his life over to the care and will of God. Come on! The man carried a gun in his Bible like Buck and the preacher with a bat in the trunk of his car like Joe Clark.

Sharon lured the intoxicated Bishop discreetly out the door and down the hall to another reserved hotel room where she completely undressed him and sat on his crotch; when the reverend finished with the word, he put his underwear on backward and hurried from the hotel! When he finally made it home, his wife discovered his underwear on backward! She thought nothing of it because it happens all the time. She thought he was just getting a taste of that forgetful disease called Alzheimer.

Hum! Fast-forwarding to Dino and Do Good in the penitentiary! While there, they were lucky to get a cell together. The system makes every good effort to pair inmates together that get along well. The fewer infractions, the better! The guards, too, want to go home after a day's work without incident, being accidental or deliberately stabbed by some crazy, disgruntled maniac. Dino took a trade in small engine repair while Do Good worked in the laundry so they would not have to pay to get their clothes cleaned and pressed. To take care of themselves, they ran stores two-for-one selling cigarettes, coffee, tuna, sardines, cakes, cookies, soda, crackers—basically everything the institution's store sold, they sold. During recreation, they would play all the sports, shoot dice, and play poker; plus, they worked out in the gym to maintain that rock-hard body.

They both called Mike and Jerry constantly, trying to stay on top of current events. Mike told Dino that he and Jerry had purchased a number of properties since they've been in prison—ten homes in the price range of 50 to 150 thousand dollars. They knew from conversation that once released from prison, it would be all good. Every day they would walk the yard discussing their future game plan once they returned home, planning unambiguously how they wanted to execute! One thing for certain: they both knew it wouldn't be wise to come out wearing flamboyant attires, flashy cars, and ridiculous jewelry—it only attracts negative attention; they learned that the hard way. Two "time" or three times warrants serving 85 percent of their time under the violent offender act and/or the three-strike law, decided by the judge having jurisdiction! That would be devastating! A real bummer.

Neither of them smoked cigarettes, but they loved smoking that "Kush"! Some of the best weed you can buy. They had money on their books. They had made a pretty decent earnings selling dope before getting caught. Every day in prison was a hunt for a weed connect. One day Joe got it, and the next day Willie got it.

It was always a witch hunt, but it was always there, secreted in the cracks of the prison walls. A good connection spells relief living among the dead in a condemned environment! Windows busted out, toilets don't work, rats as big as possums, bugs that actually fly, food degrading! You have deranged maniacs sentenced to serve life terms assigned to prepare your food; it's Murphy's Law in prison—"what can happen, will happen." It's a danger zone, a land mine for human beings. Prisons are schools for thieves; you only get worse, but of course, there's always that rare exception to the rule.

Dino was sharing with his brother as they walked the track, "Man, do you realize we are like the walking dead," living in a medieval, barbaric world, told what to do from sunrise till midnight. Jerry replied, "Nothing but a number—that's what we are! But you know, there are lessons in this experience. What you say we get us a domino game?"

"Yeah! That sounds like a good idea."

Back home, Mike and Jerry decided there's no need to continue working for Mr. Banks! At the end of the day, the plan was to tell him they wanted to resign from Pleasant Island Resort due to growth in their real estate business. Looking out the window from the refreshment store onto the golf course, the golfers appeared to be following the ball as it flew through the air, kind of chuckling as one put his driver back into its bag. "I wonder," said Jerry, "can this be what I think it is?" The moment Jerry entertained the thought, he followed the direction they were looking in—and cling went grandma's window. They, too, smiled, knowing the exact reason why this accident happened. Poor grandma!

Mike and Jerry's day had come to an end, walking down the hall to Banks's office to give him the news; here it is! A knock on the door.

"Come in," said Mr. Banks!

As they crossed the threshold walking into his office, they noticed in an adjoining office with the door slightly ajar Starlet wearing a short, short royal blue skirt with a tiny white top that exposed her cleavage and belly button. She's hot! Jerry didn't really go there because of the relationship he has with Mike's sister. But to himself, he said, "Damn. She's fine!"

Banks grabbed their attention, "What can I do for you? Need another loan?"

"No, Mr. Banks," said Mike and Jerry. Mike continued, "We just came in to get your blessings for our request to resign because our real estate has grown and became more demanding. It's getting kind of difficult to maintain both obligations. We want to still enjoy the opportunity to come out and swim, golf, horse ride, and the other amenities as well! We understand in normal circumstances you have to become a member of the resort and not a visitor to gain full and exclusive access to certain attractions you offer."

Banks responded, "Well, fellas, I wouldn't want to hold you hostage when you have promising careers ahead of you. Yes! You have my blessings! However, I need you guys to stick around for a spell to allow time for me to replace the two of you. The replacements are going to be hard because you are a really great team! Nonetheless, can you stay for one more week?"

"Sure," said Mike and Jerry!

Chapter 10

Samantha thumbed through her Rolodex to find Wiggins' number, going right to it as though it were meant for this phone call. It had been two weeks since their last conversation! The phone was ringing! Her mind was overwhelmed with thoughts of what to say—it had been two weeks. Something told her, just tell him the truth. With the election campaign, the girls, and the telecommunication responsibilities, things had been really hectic.

"Hello! How may I help you?"

"This is Samantha. Can I speak with Mr. Wiggins, please?"

"I'm sorry, Samantha, he's away on business at Monsanto, giving a presentation on problem-identifying and problem-solving in your area. Will you leave a message?"

"Never mind; I'll call his cell."

Calling his cell anxiously, the phone rang, and he noticed her name appear.

"Hi, sweetheart! How have you been? That was a long week."

"I know—it's been two weeks since we last talked, but I have been really busy. You know how my schedules sometimes run. I had the election campaign to organize, preparing presentations, making promises," she smiled, "and my primary obligations to the telecommunication company and all its branches."

"Yeah, sure. I do understand the inner workings of your responsibility. Samantha, I got to say, you have been constantly playing around in my head, creating major distractions at all times of the day and night! Since you're in my neck of the woods, is it possible I can see you to pick up where we left off? I won't say finish because this saga never ends!"

Ralph smiled and said, "How can I decline a memorable invitation from such a wonderful go-getter like yourself that I will cherish for a lifetime! You are amazing!"

It was an unexpected invitation, but one he would never turn down.

"Where are you staying?"

"I'm staying at the Holiday Inn closest to the airport in Orlando."

"Oh! That's just minutes away from where I am. I'll stop by around 7 o'clock. What room?"

"I'm in room 1192 in the penthouse. I'm looking forward to it. I'll see you then!"

At 6:55 p.m., Samantha pulled into the private parking garage in a teal green 2010 Bentley, wearing black heels with a soft light green summer dress, vaguely revealing the true essence of her undergarments. Victoria's Secret was not really a secret in Samantha's book. She strode gracefully, accenting her dress that clung to her nicely contoured body.

The first knock at the door—it instantly opened. Ralph knew she'd be on time, so at that precise moment, he opened the door, whether she was there or not. He knew Samantha! She was there, but she expected the same in return—a self-sufficient, very assertive woman! Steak dinners were the order, with Patron and orange juice as the drink of the evening. After dinner, she cuddled briefly under Ralph, making small talk but seductively persuading him to change course!

With Ralph exploring every inch of her sensual body, gently caressing every intricate detail! The clothes began to fall to the floor as they entered the bedroom. Another wild night to remember! The chemistry was there! Every opportunity, they would meet and enjoy each other. Their wealth was astronomical, with absolutely no perimeter or ceiling to how far they could go! They were extremely ambitious and always encouraging. Carol and Sherry gave up their jobs as a physical therapist and hotel manager at the Holiday Inn; with 15 properties between the two of them on the market under Section 8, all currently occupied.

At first, they contemplated buying two cars but knew the smart thing to do would be to buy a truck to transport tools more conveniently. Mike purchased a 2009 Dodge Ram 2500 pickup, and Jerry bought a 2010 Toyota Camry! They knew strength was in numbers and knew exactly where to get help to rehab the homes. Early in the morning, they would wake up and go sit in front of the temporary agency and have guys fill out applications for hire to fix up homes. In no time, they had more workers than they needed, paying them minimum wage with no benefits unless they were licensed!

When the temporary agency finally opened its doors that morning, very few people stood out front; they employed eight people that morning! The plan worked like a charm… turning two houses out in one week's time was excellent. Working four people together as a team allowed quick turnover. "This is the way to go," said Mike. "How come we didn't think of this before?"

"Check out the temporary agency! We were on our way to buy, lease out, or sell houses with no signs of stopping anytime soon; two humble young brothers who only want to get ahead to provide a comfortable lifestyle for themselves and their future offspring!" Deciding to take another vacation, they took off for the Bahamas to have fun.

Sherry said, "That's a fantastic idea!" She was a nymphomaniac who always wanted sex, no matter what time of day or night. She couldn't wait. Once they made it to the Bahamas at the Bombay Resort and found the condo, Sherry's clothes fell off with the "Do Not Disturb" sign on the door. It seemed like when she vacations, she gets this aura that makes her twice as freaky; "This is the opportunity I've been waiting for," she said, shutting the bedroom door! We can only imagine what went on behind closed doors. All I know is the "Do Not Disturb" sign stayed on the door for quite a while.

Interruption! The phone rings! Sherry picks up the phone, Mike on the other end; "Are you guys ready to surf the town and see what the Bahamas really entail?" They had just finished having their moment.

"Yeah!" she replied. "We'll meet you guys out front in ten minutes." They went into hot clubs, one after the other, having fun. Clubs there are much different than the ones in New York; tourists from four corners of the universe, speaking in many different languages! You may not be able to distinguish what they are saying, but they certainly understood that magical universal language (music). Later that evening, as the momentum slowed, they noticed a restaurant with girls wearing grass skirts and men in diapers caught their attention, so they went in and sat down to eat. Carol took pictures to save and share priceless memories of their trip to the Bahamas!

Two days before leaving, they went to the beach to get that Bahamas suntan. Mike, Carol, and Jerry were reluctant, but not Sherry—ambitious and ready to go. She strutted across the sand in her little scandalous two-piece, unable to wait to take it all off. Though she acts incredibly wild, Jerry was the one person who understood her; she absolutely loved to flirt consensually yet provocatively, showcasing her attractive body!

Running nonstop since the plane touched down, they decided, "Let's go back to the hotel and relax for a spell." The next morning, they boarded the plane and headed back home. Mike asked Jerry if he wanted to go to Grandma's house once they arrived back in town.

Jerry replied, "Yeah! That's cool!" Once the plane landed, they picked up the baggage and departed the airport, heading home and dropping the girls off before they hit the interstate. Forty minutes later, Grandma's doorbell rang. She opened the door, excited to see Mike and Jerry. Mike wanted to go horseback riding, so he dragged Jerry along for the ride. That's what friends do!

When they got back to the condo, Mike sat down and started talking with Grandma. Jerry interrupted, asking Mike if he wanted to go swimming before it got too late. Mike replied, "No! I'm going to stay here with Grandma." It was 8 o'clock. The lighting around the pool wasn't great; they resembled dimmer lights. There were about eight other condos in the immediate area. The lights from the porches of the condos didn't cast good light either. He couldn't help noticing Starlet sitting out on the balcony all alone, catching a breath of fresh air.

She obviously heard the splash in the pool. Curiosity told her to get her binoculars from the dresser drawer to get a better visual! Usually, there is no moonlight entertainment in the pool unless there is a party! She had no idea who this was because Banks had friends over for the weekend. As she gained vivid focus, spotting Jerry climb out of the pool, biceps bulging as he dried his face with that sexy ripple-effect washboard abs, she licked her lips, thinking, "What a gorgeous body!" Taste buds peaking! She hurried to get undressed, wearing only a towel, evenly balanced, that barely covered the top and bottom portion of her most prized possessions. When she approached the pool, walking out of the darkness into the light, Jerry took a double take.

"Hi! What's a girl doing out on a night like this all alone, wearing next to nothing?" Before he could get the word "nothing" out of his mouth, her towel dropped to the ground as she dove into the pool. Jerry couldn't do anything but shake his head as she submerged in the water. "Wow! Am I dreaming?" Suddenly, she gracefully emerged to his feet, and her head popped out of the water wearing that aura— "I'm ready if you are" face. Looking right at his crouch, Starlet said, "I told you I might not be wearing anything. That's the only comfortable way to swim."

"At my estate, there is absolute privacy, and I take a swim two, three times a week. What's your reason here?"

"I'm Mr. Banks' bookkeeper and personal consultant. My name is Starlet Templeton!"

"And your name is?" she asked.

"My name is Jerry! I used to work in the maintenance department, the golf course, the refreshment stand—you name it. This was just a few months ago! Why did you terminate?"

"Well! A friend and I, whose grandma so happened to own one of the condos, decided to step out on faith, take an improvised adventure into the world of real estate. We buy foreclosed homes, renovate, rent, lease, and sell. We are humble and blessed to be able to continue coming out to the resort and enjoy all the fringe benefits."

"How often do you swim here? You have a very sexy body with an equally attractive personality."

Samantha replied, "Maybe twice a week; it depends on my schedule."

Sherry was starting to worry, so Jerry tactfully concluded their conversation with closing remarks: "Hopefully, I can catch you at the pool again sometime."

Starlet replied, "Yeah, why not! Maybe you can catch me somewhere else too if your timing's right." They both smiled as she bit her bottom lip!

Chapter 11

The next day, Rita McDonald, secretary for the Supreme Court judge and former girlfriend of Banks, out of the blue, decided to call. They were an item prior to his wife, who recently passed due to cancer; since then, he hadn't found interest in a woman, at least on a serious level! Margie's passing really took something out of him. Rita was a bore to him because she always talked about the court and snored loud when she slept—annoying! Very good looking, but bad chemistry! Banks was a criminal, and court conversations didn't turn him on. Finally, he transferred over to pick up.

"Hello! Rita, how have you been? The last time I saw you, you were in St. Louis." Thinking to himself, I wonder how many boyfriends she ran off in the past ten years. Rita responded, "I'm excellent! I called to see how things have been going for you since the passing."

"Well, I've been dating a young lady by the name of Starlet Templeton. An exhibitionist, innovative and exciting in every way! She's the boss in the streets and the boss in the sheets! You know Howell! Well, he's the one who made our acquaintance. Actually, he referred her to me to conduct an investigation; I won't go into details, but that's when the relationship just happened. On the first initial interview, we made a connection that words cannot convey. We sometimes go out to fun places, lunch and dinner engagements, horseback riding, swimming, movies—things of that nature."

Rita interrupted, "What you say I come out this weekend and spend my vacation there?"

"Well, Rita," he said, "you know there's always a condo available for you. You're my friend! However, unfortunately, I will be really busy this weekend and won't get an opportunity to spend any time with you; big business deals are on the table that has to be chiseled out before the start of the next work week! Boy!" he said, "She's really making it difficult."

"Bob! I think instead I'll just postpone until a later day and spend time with Mom. I'm sure there'll be more opportunities to spend time." Banks exhaled with relief! Off the hook!

"How's your mom doing?"

"She's okay! Still dealing with her heart troubles, one day at a time, taking a daily aspirin and all the other medications prescribed."

"Yeah! I know how that is! God has his arms wrapped around her with his enormous blessings that will fill a pool. She is in good hands! We just have to trust in the Lord. Ask him for the favor and leave it where it is; otherwise, you question his will. We cannot move in doubt! But instead, blind faith! The unseen! Maybe next month will be a much better time considering we're booked up for the rest of this month."

Rita agreed; the timing was bad, and next month would be better. The conversation concluded! Rita was introspectively disappointed with the outcome!

A month later, Mike and Jerry had 25 homes and were now contemplating office space to set up shop for business. Plus, they knew changes had to be made regarding whether they wanted to continue carpeting the floors for tenants under Section 8 or resort to floor tile that would be more economical. "Cut out the bad small section and install the new, and you're ready to go!"

Moreover, giving thought to the style of painting; the two or three different colors usually supplied is time-consuming, with a greater chance that flaws can be more easily revealed! Mike also mentioned the need for supervisors to orchestrate the workers' assignments; the reason for the need for a supervisor was it gives more time to find homes to buy and sell! Carol and Sherry put an ad in the paper for supervisors in the field of home renovation and a professional (guru) business consultant who understands the business as it's written! "We really need to get more vigilant in our endeavors to be the best in the business; in a horse race, the horse with the most incentive wins!"

The next day, Carol and Sherry received over 50 phone calls for interviews; all interviews were scheduled for Thursday and Friday the next week. The grueling interviews were finally over. They hired a young man, 35, named Jonathan Jones, and a young lady, 27, by the name of Mrs. Darlene Sims, licensed in the field of electrical engineering, plumbing, and carpentry. They were also lucky enough to find an old guru named George Robinson, who knew the business like the back of his hand! He came to them through an AARP program that offers assistance to any startup business to help get them up and running at no expense; you couldn't beat that! Many years ago, George took a brilliant course in quality circles that teach problem identification and problem solving. He had four years of college studying business management and accounting for a business manager position at Ralston Purina, accountant for Colgate

Toothpaste, and troubleshooting specialist for Gun Decker Realtors; he was overqualified, and that's what we wanted.

The same day, on the mean streets of New York, just as the special task force disrobed their suit of armor because all possible leads had seemingly dried up like a prune, even the painters were clueless. We know all painters aren't reliable, especially when a favor is not owed to an officer for conveniently dropping the ball to get them off the hook in exchange for information. At that precise moment, the Red Light Machete Bandit struck again!

Breaking news interruption! The fire department, police department, news media helicopter, news coverage on the ground, ambulance, and witnesses were all over the place, watching this tragic scene. The news media explained what they'd been told to update the viewers! What happened here approximately five minutes ago? Witnesses and victims who were being transported to the hospital said while the guy stood at the gas island pumping his gas, they assumed a hooded person appeared from nowhere, walked up behind the guy pumping the gas, and wham! Cut his hand off while holding the pump. His hand fell to the ground, along with the hose that was cut from the blow. Gas simultaneously spilled to the pavement! The victim was petrified, frozen still from panic, with a cigarette hanging on his bottom lip as though it were stuck, then seconds later, falling to the ground, setting off a huge fire! While this was taking place, the guy ran very quickly, darting across the street, vanishing into the wooded area like a sly fox.

The poor guy who lost his hand caught on fire; he ran away from the pumps, fell down, and began rolling until the fire dissipated! It really wasn't until then that I noticed the man's hand had been cut completely off. It was bleeding profusely, and he was holding his wrist! "There you have it, folks! This is really scary! I'm in awe that the police department can't catch this deranged madman."

"We must maintain our vigilance; we'll catch this guy. We're signing off for now from News Channel 4. We will definitely keep you thoroughly up to date on any developments in this case!" While this chaos festered, I made a call to the special task force supervisor to see if he caught the news flash. He replied, "I'm looking at it now! We're on it! This guy is insane! We have to stop him like yesterday." He called his team in and told them to contact everyone that witnessed the crime and put every painter we have back on the streets.

"We have to put the pressure on to get this fish out of the water! John, make sure when you get to the scene, you secure that surveillance footage!" When John got there, he rushed in to review the footage, and unfortunately, the camera was compromised due to bad lighting! Several lights underneath the gas island had blown. The cameras didn't respond very well. "Damn!" John said. "This guy is lucky enough to s—t in a swinging jug!" John retrieved the video and took it back to the station.

Watching very closely, he noticed this guy had the same build as the one-armed guy named Eugene who left the hospital without permission. "Look at him as he runs across the street, navigating his way through the wooded area like a lion in his natural habitat! When drugs alter your mind, you never know to what extent you'll go until you're there. This guy is off the chain! He is definitely suicidal! This is the straw! The board of Probation and Parole will repudiate every effort he makes to get parole. A mental institution is bound to step in if he's ever released from custody.

"He'll probably be there for the rest of his life! Drug use is a deadly disease that cannot be controlled by man if consumed. Don't fool yourself!"

A few blocks away, Jerry and Mike concluded their interview, turning on the TV in the office, witnessing a fire at a familiar service station. He told Sherry to hold up for a minute; she was talking over the news broadcast. "Look!" he said. "This guy has cut off somebody else's hand at the Amoco service station around the corner at the red light; only this time he managed to contribute to blowing up the whole damn lot. Man!"

"Dang! That guy blows my mind," Mike responds. "That's crazy! But you know, Jerry, to turn the page, we have to make our work trucks available to them and go out and buy something different for ourselves." The two of them went and bought brand new cars.

Chapter 12

The following week, they went to an auction and successfully bid on a sixteen-unit apartment complex that only cost them 120 thousand dollars; anticipating that with the sharpshooters hired, the sixteen units would be ready in three months. Three bedrooms and one bath.

That evening after work, Jerry decided to take a shower, play around with Sherry, and watch some gangster romantic videos. Mike and Jerry had also purchased two homes for themselves with two bedrooms and two baths from HUD; they renovated them and moved in.

Living that lavish lifestyle was spoken into existence. Every home purchased was undeniably gorgeous, and in no time someone was moving in. Upgrading the neighborhood became a passion, knowing they were actually playing a serious game of Monopoly to consume a particular amount of properties to gain control and political clout. Mike went to the post office to get his mailing address changed, and the first piece of mail received was from guess who?

Mr. Gary Henson, AKA Dino! The letter was from Attica State Prison and it read,

"Seasons Greetings! Hi Mike! The parole board granted Do Good and me another chance; 'Do Good gets out one week before me.' I get out on the 18th of September and he gets out on the 10th of September 2010. They stipulated we had to have a good home and job plan. You know we can always go back home to moms. We just need you guys to look out for us; we need employment; last time we quite obviously didn't have our heads on right. This time it'll be different! Write back and tell us something!" Right away, Mike sat down and began writing a scribe back to Dino, explaining things had been going swell for them and that he was going to have Carol write a letter to the board assuring that you guys will have jobs once released from prison! That they own a real estate company that purchases houses monthly and renovations are perpetual.

Do Good was released on a Monday and Dino was released the following Monday. When they touched down, Jerry and Mike gave fifteen hundred dollars to each of them to buy clothes for themselves; they knew they still had money but that it was a token of their appreciation for a job well done! Extrication from that place is a breath of fresh air. To see and touch a woman's flesh is phenomenally out of this world. Dino called his girlfriend, but she was at work. He called her job and she picked up!

Tabitha was extremely excited to hear his voice. "Baby, I can't wait to get off work. Where are you going to be?" "I'll be here at mom's house when you get off." Impatiently watching the clock! The minute the clock struck 5 o'clock, she was out the door rushing to the car and down the street she went. They tore the bedroom up, overwhelmed with the idea that neither of them had sex in about a year.

His mother heard vividly through the paper-thin walls the explicit language and the shaking of the wall, and the pictures periodically shook. She knew what was going to happen when Tabitha got off work.

They hadn't intimately touched one another in one year. Dino came home the following week! Walking out of the prison gates, stretching and giving thanks to God for another chance due to the overcrowding in the system; his girlfriend left him for another guy because she said he stays in and out of jail too much and they could never establish anything real or tangible together because he acquires it with a suicidal attempt to return to prison. In other words, she didn't want a life with a guy who always flinches and looks over his shoulder when a siren suddenly goes off when the police are in pursuit of someone or sometimes ducking when police do a drive-by at night, flashing a light through your window to make sure you're safe in your home. Dino didn't let that bother him. He knew right where to go to get relief.

On the corner where all the hookers hang out; he first pulled into a store to get some vodka and juice and a pack of Trojan horse protection because he knew he wasn't going skin diving with all the diseases running rampant through the hood; no way! Now he heads to the corner where all the honeys parade back and forth until a trick pulls them over. I guess Dino was the trick that day because he had to explode somewhere, and it wasn't going to be in his hand today; they all looked good! He didn't know which one to pick, so he grabbed two girls and said, "Let's go have some fun." One black and the other white, the best of both worlds! "What are your names?" he said!

The sister replied, "My name is Sugar! What's yours?" The white girl said, "My name is Fantasy! I go where other women refuse to go." Dino replied, "Get in the car." In route to find the nearest cheap hotel; coming up on a Best Western; it wasn't the best by far, but Dino planned to spend two days with these ladies. He didn't care what the cost! Two days later, finally emerging, he felt relieved from the mounting pressure! Dino dropped the ladies off and headed for home. When he walked through the door, Do Good and his mother asked, "Where have you been? You were released two days ago; we were worried about you." His mother, shaking her head, said, "Don't tell me! I know exactly where you were! We thought you had gotten locked back up and created a scene and weren't allowed to make a call." He replied, "I'm sorry!

I had unfinished business." "Boy! Whatever happened to coming home first?" "Momma, you know pressure burst pipes, and mine was screaming for justice." Smiling, "Gone boy," said his mother.

They were told that they had to report every two weeks with check stubs and every so often unexpectedly, they'd have to give a urine analysis to determine whether they were walking the straight and narrow! Guns in the home were an automatic violation; and if they decided to move, the parole office had to be informed within 24 hours. Do Good was already working for Mike and Jerry, and Dino was employed the next three days after he'd arrived home! Jerry and Mike decided not to put the two brothers together because it might slow down production, so they put them under different supervision. They didn't know much about the business but were eager to learn with no other jobs available to turn to; Gary and Harvey were very impressive! They caught on exceptionally fast. Enthusiastic, jovial, and possessed an outstanding perspicacity that was absolutely remarkable. Dino and Do Good had contemplated going into the same business venture once their capital was right. That was the reason they adjusted so easily!

During break, Dino asked Jerry when they would put them back in pocket. Jerry replies! It's been a while since they last picked up some, and the only thing they concentrated on was real estate! But I'll tell you what! Give yourselves a little more time to recuperate from the exhausting stay in prison. Plus, you guys need a chance to reacquaint yourselves with the streets; people that weren't painting before are painters now. The movement in the police department and distinguishing a good spot to set up shop as opposed to a bad spot! There are variables you might consider before taking that risk. Dino agrees by nodding his head and saying, "You're right man! Patience is important."

"No problem! I'll tell Do Good in about two weeks things will be right."

Two weeks had passed; they went back to the resort to look around, feeling the vibrations and the aura in the air! Although everything should be okay, it's always safe to check first. Jerry was anxious to go anyway because he thought Starlet might coincidentally pop up at the pool again! He couldn't discard her from his mind. Unfortunately, she was away on business.

He did happen to bump into Mr. Eckert, the private investigator. "Hi, Jerry!" said Eckert! "I haven't sent you guys around in a while. Mr. Banks told me that the two of you went into business for yourselves; how's the business coming along?" "Great," said Jerry! "I'll see you around; enjoy your swim." Eckert turned and walked away. Meantime, Mike just closed the cabinet, taking one key of cocaine! A little bit nervous because it's been a long time since the last caper; plus, there is the mixed emotion because they really didn't have to continue to steal from Mr. Banks! Now they're trying to accommodate Dino and Do Good but still make money for themselves. Anytime you do things for the wrong reasons, it comes back to bite you right in the butt. An hour later, Jerry returned from his swim, shivering and kind of pale: the indoor heated pool is nice. It has a high dive most indoor pools don't have. Mike quickly changed the subject! "Man, I was nervous this time!"

"Jerry curious! Why so nervous this time?" "It's not so much the fear of getting caught; we've come so far, and things are looking up for us. We don't need to continue taking unnecessary chances like this anymore." "What's the big deal?" Jerry said. "We don't involve ourselves with the distribution of the product; that's Dino and Do Good's responsibility. We're not taking the risk!" "I don't know about that," said Mike. "Every time we move anything anywhere, we are taking a chance. I guess it's just my gut feeling talking to me; I'm sure you have those moments yourself when something doesn't feel right."

Chapter 13

Three months had passed since the purchase of the sixteen units; both supervisors walked into Mike and Jerry's office with the good news: the sixteen units are complete and they're ready for the next project. Nothing better than a plan that comes together without glitches to slow progress! "What do you say we surprise our supervisors with an incentive bonus package for the Christmas holidays for a job?" "That is a good idea! Why not!" "Okay! Now that that's settled, what do you say we keep them working on the five homes we purchased last week until December 20th, 2024?" "Okay! That sounds like a winner. Now that the real estate business is off the table, how do you want to deal with Dino and Do Good?"

They've shown impeccable loyalty ever since we have known them; why don't we give them 36 ounces with the understanding that 12 ounces belong to them and the other 24 belong to us? All they have to do is bring to the storehouse 24 thousand dollars at one thousand per ounce; the stuff takes a six, so you know they're going to step on it at least once before they serve it.

"It's a deal! Call Dino!" They've been waiting patiently for this. Ring, ring! Do Good answers the phone! "Hello! Who's calling?" "This is Mike, playa! We're ready when you guys are! Is Dino around?" "No, he's not! He just left with his new girlfriend. Let me call him and tell him you called. Where's the spot you want us to meet?" "The old spot! Johnnie's house!" John was a drug addict they all knew since childhood. He was the tester to determine the drugs' potency. "Meet us there at 6:00 o'clock straight up."

"It's a deal!" At 6:00 o'clock, Dino and Do Good had been there for 15 minutes, sitting in front of the house; dropping the package off, they were told to be careful; snakes are squirming all over the place! We don't want that same precarious situation to happen again. Do Good and his brother looked at each other and said, "Man, it's a blessing to have a good connect. They knew much more could be made from that package. Chances are we'll make the same thing they make, if not more."

Mike and Jerry weren't concerned about that because they didn't have to purchase the merchandise; it was free! "I don't know about that!" Jerry said in parting; "Just give us a jingle when you guys are finished." Though it was a little rough this time, they knew what they had because they had John to sample the goods! Johnnie confirms it's the bomb!

This stuff takes your breath away…The reason they didn't sell the stuff as fast as before was because most of them had either gotten locked up or gotten killed. Compliments of the game! It was a totally different clientele of folks out there; new faces meant a much higher risk. New faces and swagger can sometimes be difficult to read. When you think you are dealing with a stomp-down thoroughbred, you are dealing with a lame horse that should have been put out of its misery because he's in agony and pain and willing to compromise anything to get that drug to feel better! He doesn't care who the sacrificial lamb is; he wants what he wants and he wants it now! He's a painter, an undercover cop! He could be tact, scat, or the FBI! As the days progressed and the paper chase got greater, they gravitated back to the club, meeting different women and rolling the dice; they knew drugs and violence complemented one another; deceit is also a part of that dangerous ingredient as well! Drug addicts always try to figure out how they can manipulate or set you up to be robbed. Dino and Do Good really weren't brothers you want to have bad blood with; they would go to any extreme with pernicious and diabolical unimaginable tactics.

Their minds were concealed lethal weapons! Their hands were lethal; that is what kept them on top of the game; dope addicts paged them all night long, didn't bother them in the least! It was a money call… When it went off, out the door they went full throttle; offers came to them that were unbelievable; clothing, shoes, jewelry, houses, cars, boats, trucks, and women selling sex for a grain of crack; they would use any kind of provocative approach to lure you in.

Addicts just cannot do without their deadly enticing mood-altering chemical that could snuff out a life in a fleeing second. Death on an installment plan that you never see coming, like the Republicans and Democrats assassinating themselves!

Early one Sunday morning, Do Good got a page. Dino was still in bed. He assumed it was a young lady named Linda who he, on occasion, takes to the hotel. When he returned the page, he found out it was just a wrong number. Someone had coincidentally used his code. Dino briefly spoke with him. Larry told him that he was with another guy who had dealings with him earlier that week! Dino decided to go against his better judgment and accept the invitation to meet. That's when he learned to set up his own meeting places. From that point forward, he convinced Do Good to meet with him in an old abandoned building where he was ambushed, shot in the leg, and robbed! Crawling out of a vacant house, pulling himself into his car,

Do Good drove to the hospital. Upon arrival, the intake asked him his name, next of kin, and a phone number where someone could be reached. He replied! "My name is Harvey Henson; my mother's name is Hattie Henson and the phone number is 261-4364." The hospital, without delay, notified his mother and told her that Harvey had been shot in the leg. Before he could say anything else, she and Dino were out the door, headed straight to the hospital!

A good chess player thinks three moves in advance. The money grossly impaired his vision! It persuaded him to take a grave risk with the odds totally against him; he conveniently forgot to play by the rudiments of the mean streets; next time, it could be worse. When they made it to the hospital, Dino asked him what happened! He told him this guy named Larry lured him into a vacant building; a guy came from behind out of the scope of his peripheral vision and stuck a gun in his rib. Took one hundred dollars and an ounce of "girl," and they both ran. I crawled out of the vacant building and pulled myself up in the car.

"I remember the faces! We'll meet again and it'll be my turn. I'm going to break both their necks!" Two days later, signing himself out of the hospital without release. The doctor told him if he signed out, that would relieve the hospital of any liabilities. He left! His mother nursed him back to health. Months passed and he hadn't seen those guys nowhere but the memory would never fade. That lesson keeps him on his toes. He now thinks about that day in question every time he makes a transaction with anybody!

Dino called Mike and Jerry to tell them what happened. They were stunned at the news but excited to know he was alright. They stopped in anyway to see how he was doing. Do Good was okay! Just upset with him for going for the bait. While Mike and Jerry were contemplating whether now was the right time to give them the key so that they could sell it, Banks discovered the snake had returned back to the garden. Another key was missing!

Immediately, he called Eckert into his office; "Bob, he's back! Another key has just come up missing; there must be something we can do to expeditiously resolve this problem." Introspectively, he thought, "I have to inform Starlet about this matter." Bob still didn't suspect she was not only hired to help him investigate the incident but intrude in his life as well to find out if he's connected in some way!

He thought Bob was sabotaging the investigation! The last time this occurred was the week Eckert took his vacation to Florida. Now, nearly one year later, it happens again. Eckert quietly thought, "Robert never loses his composure no matter what."

"Robert," he replies! "I do understand how much this means to you and me as well; I will get to the bottom of it," speaking with invigorating confidence! Bob then excused himself from his office. Minutes later, he called Starlet Templeton into his office and explained to her his expectations from this juncture forward; she was given specific orders to note everybody coming and leaving Ms. Reid's home! I mean a fully fledged report on everybody, including Bob Eckert.

"I am appalled this thief is still lurking around. It is creating chaos! He'll fumble, and when he does, I'll be right there to catch it. Starlet, I must say hiring you to investigate has really impeded our quality time together, but I guess that is the way it has to be for now; if you were never hired to help with this investigation, I probably wouldn't have met you!"

The entire time Robert was talking, she was sitting on the edge of his desk, wearing a bone-white pair of slacks, one hundred percent cotton, complemented with a soft green button-up top revealing a sign of cleavage! Bob couldn't resist planting a subliminal message; "Every time we're together, my mouth waters like I'm eating Starburst. What do you think that is?" Starlet gazed into his eyes and saw a look that was irresistible; he was biting his lip in anticipation; one foot barely on the floor, the other leg kind of swinging back and forth as she unbuttoned her top, then she started to unzip her pants down partway, unveiling a sexy tattoo that says "juicy."

Chapter 14

Robert mesmerized her with his slow-motion foreplay as Starlet started to gently touch her {G spot} and put her finger in her mouth. "Watching this, I couldn't help being sexually aroused; poker obviously wasn't my strong suit here." She really surprised Banks when she took her hand out of her lower region and said, "Taste me! Delicious, isn't it?" Then smiles! Before he could respond, her finger was in his mouth! "I get wet from the mere thought of you…" Seductively turning her back to him as though she was correcting her attire! Robert, standing behind her, wrapped his arms around her and gently gravitated downwards to her tender spot, fondling sensually; he pulled her back to him on the desk! A paperweight fell to the floor, growing hard, but his Calvin Klein briefs lived up to its reputation, holding him down not to appear too aroused. He decides to exercise his better judgment and pass until later that evening; Robert certainly didn't want to compromise his objectives or fundamental principles supplied in the workplace.

Starlet paused, feeling the vibe! She said, "I'll savor this irresistible temptation until tonight!" Robert pulls it together and calls Samantha to see if her shipment had come in. The telephone rings several times before the receptionist picks up. "Hello! This is Veronica! How may I direct your call?" "This is Robert Banks at the New York area location." "Yes! How are you?" "I'm good, thanks! Hold for a sec, please." She has someone on another line; she'll be right with you! "Hi, Robert! I was just chatting with Ralph on the other line; you and Ralph have really gotten close lately; I'm glad for you! The reason I called is because a shipment of 'No Huff NO PUFF' would be arriving." She knew as a general rule no questions asked: 1,500 keys of cocaine were included with that drop-off.

"Yeah! As a matter of fact, they're here unloading it now in the warehouse as we speak."

"Good! I was just checking on you, sweetheart… How are the girls doing? I know their productivity as usual!" Samantha canvassed the workstation with her eyes and replied, "They're doing just fine. You should come out and see us sometime."

"I just may take you up on that, Sam," he calls her short for Samantha. "Talk to you later! Bye!"

Dino was coming along fine. He had a slight limp but it didn't bother him. He wanted to go to Flamingo "Wednesday Night Comedy"! Dino wore a long-length leather coat and Do Good wore his long-length smoke gray leather coat with a very well-articulated design that stood out in any crowd; two hours in the club, Do Good spots the guy who ambushed and robbed him.

He was seated near the front of the club. It was almost impossible to see him from the rear of the club, but Do Good had a memory like an elephant and eyes like an eagle when it came to this guy because he had robbed and assaulted him! Do Good knew if you let someone take from you without repercussions, you may as well terminate yourself from the game; and he hadn't planned on turning in his resignation anytime soon! The guy got up and headed towards the restroom; now his mind was really racing because he didn't want him to get away! "I can leave and go get strapped and wait outside for him;

I can go to the car, get a knife, and stab him to death; neither idea was good enough, so he told Dino he just saw the guy that robbed him.

"Where is he?" said Dino. "He just went in the restroom. I'll tell you what, I'll go in the restroom while you stand outside the door." "Dino! I can handle it;" Do Good walked into the restroom. The guy was standing at the urinal, relieving himself! After he finished, he turned to wash his hands, looking in the mirror; his worst nightmare! Do Good, without any hesitation, commenced "V Necking" him, choking and choking his jugular to cut off his wind; the more he resisted, the faster he went out! His hands finally went limp, uncontrollably falling to his side, but he continued to hold his lock like a pit bull a while longer to make sure he was dead instead of playing possum or temporarily unconscious; it had happened to him once before! So to make sure he went back and snapped his neck for security and lowered him to the floor, sticking his head in the toilet in one of the stalls and closed the door! Dino and his brother left the club without suspicion!

Dino asked Do Good exactly what did you do in there while they sat in the car? Smiling! he replied! "I V Necked him, snapped his neck, and stuffed his ass in the toilet." "Somebody will eventually discover his behind." They drove off in the Beemer.

Eight months later, Mike and Jerry continued their quest. They now had 30 properties. Problems were beginning to occur at the 16 units. A tenant under the Section Eight housing program had destroyed her unit, and Section Eight gave her 90 days to get the deficiencies repaired, and she dropped the ball. Tina was a crack cocaine addict, a heroin junky, and more! She had three kids with no regard for their health or well-being; a boyfriend who was lazy and wasn't legally allowed to stay due to policy and procedure prohibiting staying in the home; her entry lock was missing on the front door, and it swung open like a saloon door in John Wayne's days. Traffic all day and night! A dope fiend will cuddle with anybody and wake up the next morning without shame; if they wake up together when the sun rises! Her clothes scattered on the floor throughout the apartment; food items such as open cans of tuna, sardines, chicken, peanut butter, and on the floor, the closet, and dresser drawers destroyed; it was in complete shambles; her rent was 380.00 dollars, with Section Eight paying 367.00 dollars! She only paid 13.00 dollars out of pocket! Once they terminated her from the program, Mike and Jerry followed Section Eight's lead by telling her that her contract had expired and a renewal was not an option because she was taken off the Section Eight program. With that, she could no longer afford the monthly rent. In addition, she kept the unit in a deplorable state of shock; bugs and mice were all over the place. What actually took place was she became disgruntled once Mike told her she had to vacate the premises. Through her insidious vindictiveness, she thought cunning ways to cause harm; that was her reasoning for spreading food all over the apartment; sabotage!

She single-handedly created a devastatingly tragic situation; her plans were to intentionally offset the actual date she would be moving out of the apartment; so she would tell Mike or Jerry when they would stop by to see if she had moved, she would always say, "I'm moving next week"! They had heard it so many times they knew the court had to step in; was the only legal option, so they thought! The week they declined to stop by to see if she had vacated the premises is when they started receiving unexpected phone calls; the tenants from the other 15 units in the apartment complex all calling because their apartments suddenly had mice running all over the place! They had seized control like Ben and his boys!

Ring, ring! Mike answered the phone. "Hello! This is Mike; how can I help you?"

"This is Ashley! If you don't get someone over here to get rid of these bugs and mice like yesterday, I'm moving out!"

"I'm so sorry to hear that this has happened! I'll get over there right away."

The telephone rang again! "Hello! How may I help you? Can I speak with Mr. Garden, please?"

"Mike says! This is he! How may I help you?" She told Mike the same story as the previous caller; Mike told her that he would get on top of it ASAP. He hung up from her! He and Jerry headed that way to see how bad the problem really was. When they arrived, walking through the door of the vacant apartment the tenant had just been terminated from, they witnessed mice running across the mantelpiece, all over couches, the stove; rodents covered the floor where all this food had been randomly thrown to entice a rodent party! A job well done! Now they had to think quickly and experiment in order to make that many rats disappear in a short time. Expeditiously! So they thought about combining peanut butter with "Deacon rat poison"; they knew rats weren't drawn to Deacon alone, but they were crazy about peanut butter. They went to the store and bought two big cans of peanut butter and bags of Deacon rat poison, mixed the two together, and made little round balls, spreading them through each apartment in the hidden areas where the kids couldn't intercept! Unbelievable! All the rats had vanished like a puff of smoke. That was a huge relief to the two brothers!

Chapter 15

Two weeks later, they were back on track, but the market was shifting… The prices of the homes were not necessarily inflating, but loans were reluctant due to the strained economy. With foreclosures skyrocketing, Banks had to do their homework to make sure you qualified for the loan. The banks were under close scrutiny. It was truly a waiting game at this point! Every day scanning through the newspaper for possible leads or stumbling onto a decent piece of property through word of mouth! Buying and selling property for them was like selling drugs to Dino and his brother. It had become an addiction!

Mike and Jerry were getting a little sluggish getting packages for the Henson brothers. Signs of not keeping them supplied told the brothers something was wrong. Before they had ever let them run out of their supply, real estate had consumed them! It had absolutely nothing to do with getting supplies; the youngsters were just in a daze! Now being able finally to see a future without drugs being the primary source that carried the weight or responsibility each payroll period! They didn't have time to break away for that purpose; a two-hour run driving there and back and catching the right time to go into Banks' stash; instead of telling the Henson brothers what was going on. They were taught not to let the left hand know what the right hand was doing! So they would say "they're dead," which meant the well had dried up temporarily! A news flash! A man in Boston went into a store wheeling a machete asking for money; Mr. Henderson immediately got a description… The perpetrator had both his limbs! Pure coincidence!

Dino and Do Good were impatient; they had to keep moving. They went to Troy, a high roller who smartly stayed under the radar and loved to roll the dice! Troy sold them three ounces of cocaine. The understanding was to break the packages down into quarters just so that they could stay on track until Mike and Jerry showed through; the parole officers cut them no slack! Rigid! Getting a phone call to come into the office because they were temporarily laid off due to work stagnation; the longer an ex-felon lay down, the greater the chances were he'd become complacent and become dependent! Now the double whammy!

Upon their re-entry back into the prison system, they met two young brothers notorious for making a come-up by kidnapping a dope dealer, taking his money and dope, then killing him. The grapevine said Dino and Do Good were doing well! So they both decided to look them up after being out for two weeks. Everything started to fall in place for Big Will and Corky; they spotted Do Good at a 7 Eleven picking up a few items! Following him from a distance right to his home; patiently they waited down the street and looked who stepped out the door, Dino! He walked straight to his car, got in, and pulled off. Staying at a distance, creeping through the hood, he pulled into a driveway, got out of the car, walked up to the door, and stuck a key in; like magic, they found out where they both stayed with no complications.

Now that they knew where they lived, they had to figure out a plan to take them out; Dino and his brother still felt an adrenaline rush and a euphoria that had them in a cloud; running drugs for weeks nonstop without spending quality time with their queens, and that was important. So Do Good said, "Let's go to Club Manhattan tonight and kick it."

"Hey!" Dino replied! "Let's do that, bro. But you know we have to meet with Troy tonight at 8:30 pm to get that package."

"Well!" Do Good said! "Why don't we have our ladies meet us at the club at say 9 o'clock?"

"Cool! I'm going to call now and tell them that we got business and to meet us at the club at 9 o'clock. Hold on for a minute!"

Dino called and told them to meet them at Club Manhattan at 9 o'clock! When he called Tabitha and Shawnta, they were overcome with excitement, indecisively trying to figure out what to wear; and how they were going to have a good time! While on the same night, at the precise same time, Big Will and Corky were parked right down the street from Dino's house, plotting to make their hit.

"Oh! Wait a minute! Look, Corky! She's walking out of the house, gets in the car, and drives off; this is what we were hoping for! This is an easy score. It looks like she's going directly to Do Good's house."

"Yeah! She sure is! Pull on in there! Bingo!"

Apparently, she called her girlfriend prior to pulling up because she was walking out the door; he looked at his partner and said, "She's all mine!" Big Will pointed his finger in the direction the ladies were going and said, "Let's do this!" Not knowing where the girls were going; they were the only GPS source to lead them to Dino and Do Good. They couldn't afford to lose them! They were all in! There was no capitulation with these guys; the girls had absolutely no reason to suspect or be suspicious about anything.

Finally pulling into the parking lot at Club Manhattan, they looked in the mirror to make sure their curb appearance was sexy, got out of the car with an instant fan base; brothers trying to get off their sharp one-liners to make the girls quietly go "Wow," looking back with that sexy expression but quickly turning around and walking into the club.

Big Will said, "Ouch! That's Hot! Two gorgeous mesmerizing prize winners! Stallions! I know Dino and his brother are in the club; if not very close by.

He was right! They were already in the club. The original plan was to catch Dino and Do Good, but under the circumstances, they resorted to plan "B"—kidnap the girls and demand a ransom. The last option was great because the girls drove to the club together and hopefully they would leave together. This was their lucky day! Dino's girlfriend Tabitha walked out of the club, lit up a cigarette, and called someone on her cell phone. By this time, Corky and Big Will had become too impatient and decided to go for what they could get. They lunged from the car, flourishing a handgun, grabbed her, and threw her in the back seat, accompanied by Big Will holding a gun to her rib! Big Will told her, "Call your man! We will do the rest!"

Crying, she said, "He's not at home. He was supposed to meet us at the club, but he obviously hasn't made it yet. Call him on your cell!" She called him but didn't pick up, so she sent an urgent text to call her back immediately, that she had been kidnapped! He returned the call quickly! The phone rang; she quickly picked up. "Baby!" Before she could say anything else, Dino tried to interrupt! She insisted, "I've been kidnapped!" sobbing!

Big Will snatched the cell phone from her and demanded ten thousand dollars and five ounces of cocaine; Dino quietly thought to himself for a second, I don't have that kind of money nor cocaine. "Okay!" he replied! "Meet me at 2762 Wine Hearst Dr.; there's an old abandoned building there." This was seconds away from where they were. Calculating how much time it would take them to get Do Good situated on the roof with the .30-06 rifle with an infrared scope, he was an expert; he knew it would only take them ten minutes to set up shop. So they told the kidnappers to give him 45 minutes to pick up the money and the drugs! Big Will and Corky were very confident it would be a smooth grab and run. They knew he wouldn't do anything stupid with his girlfriend's life riding the line, so they accepted the drop-off spot he'd recommended! That was a slaughter pit where snakes were terminated!

Big Will said, "Okay, 45 minutes! Her life depends on you!" Corky kept looking at her, frantic! Constantly saying, "Please don't hurt me, please don't hurt me!" He couldn't resist the uncontrollable urge to run his hand underneath her wraparound skirt. He kept looking! Finally, he walked over to her, tied up, and ran his hand in her private area.

Tabitha kept saying, "Please don't hurt me! I'll do anything you want, just don't hurt me." The poor girl was hysterical! This was a horrifying day that would never be forgotten; Dino and Do Good knew exactly what to do. Dino was the bait, and Do Good brought the bacon home from the rooftop; the arbitrator! The executioner! Slowly turning the corner with their headlights communicating "they're coming down the dead-end street with caution"; Dino and Do Good saw them approaching the end of the block where the condemned building was located! Corky got out of the car. He looked up at the building and called out, "Dino!" Dino walked out the door and down the first flight of steps to appear to stand on a pedestal holding a bag in his hand; Do Good was excited to have two excellent shots. Big Will and Corky were both riding up front while Tabitha lay tied up in the back seat; Do Good said, "Good thinking, guys! I really appreciate your style!"

Big Will sat in the car with the engine running just in case something happened. They knew Big Will had to go down first because he had her in imminent danger. They also knew Dino had a situation on his hands because Corky stood there holding a gun! Being pros, Dino knew he had to get closer to Corky to grab his weapon. Simultaneously, Do Good would hit his man from the roof. Slowly walking down the steps towards Corky, he smooth-talked him! Getting close enough, he reached for the gun. When he grabbed it, a shot went off; leaving Dino wrestling over a gun in the street. Finally, Dino hit a sensitive pressure point on his wrist, and the gun fell to the ground, pushing him to the middle of the street. Another shot went off. Two men lay dead! The car started to roll! "Big Will's" foot pressed lightly on the accelerator; Dino ran to the car, snatched the guy out, smashed the brakes, and untied her.

Tabitha was still in mild shock, having been kidnapped by some thugs trying to kill her and her man over some drugs! She was determined not to live that lifestyle! Being a "High Roller's girl" could involve serious consequences that could result in losing a limb or a life!

She said, "It's not worth it!" It remained a mystery for a while! "Do Good" cuddled, kissed, and caressed her tender spot; sealing the deal! But the thought continued to linger! Cocaine/Murder! If Tabitha ever found out [I] got kidnapped, it would send her straight into shock! They were just innocent girls who happened to be attracted to guys with precarious distinguishing edges and moved in the super-fast lane!

Tabitha pulled herself together, and they headed back to the club. Shawnta and her girlfriends were sitting there talking and having fun; time had slipped away. She hadn't realized one hour had passed since Tabitha stepped out to smoke.

So she got up, excused herself, and walked out of the club to see if Tabitha was still outside; she was nowhere in sight! She got upset! She flipped open her cell phone and dialed Do Good's number; before the phone could ring, she noticed them pull into the parking lot.

"Shawnta!" she walked to the car, got in, and told them, "I'm pissed. That I started to catch a ride from the club because Tabitha never came back in! She stepped out to smoke! I thought something was seriously wrong. I got worried and left! What happened?"

Tabitha articulated, "They pulled up, and I jumped in and went to the liquor store to get some 'Patron' before the stores closed. Knowing later that night [we] might want another drink."

"Okay! But damn girl! You could have called me on your cell," Shawnta said.

"Girl, I know I was tripping, but it happened so fast, and I knew you were cool." No more was said. She wrote it off like Bank of America in a foreclosure!

Dino and Do Good glanced at each other and said, "Hey! What did they do?" Then smiled! Shawnta suppressed her feelings until the early next morning; before they awakened the next morning, a kid noticed two men lying dead in a ditch about 200 feet from one another!

So he hurried home to tell his mom and dad about the two dead men! They didn't bother to see the bodies rolled over in a ditch, quickly calling the police to report two dead bodies lying in a ditch at 2752 Wine Hearst Dr., which was down the street from where it took place! A notorious cavity for breeding crime, vacant and run-down houses, dope dealers, prostitution, pimps, big dice games with take-home pay as high as "50 G's" on any given night!

Chapter 16

Later that morning, Dino and Shawnta finally pulled themselves out of bed after a terrifying night that literally scared her to death; sober from the night before, out of the blue, she told Dino, "I am pissed with you because you put my life in danger! You inconsiderately took a gamble with not only your life but enjoyed the conceited luxury of taking others as well! How much was the ransom? Do you realize my life was on the line? You don't know how much pressure my heart can sustain; I was devastated! I told you I didn't want to be involved in this kind of relationship!"

Dino flashed back! "Why Dino, why? I can imagine how Tabitha would feel if she found out I'd been kidnapped; she would flip out. How come you can't sell real estate like your friends? You're just chasing your tail; you make money! You're in and out of a revolving door that continues to spin. You'll never get a chance to make a life for yourself; before you know it, you're old and no one wants to hire you because you are a liability and no longer an asset to any business; no medical benefits and reluctant to buy medicine for yourself even on a discount because the money's not there. Wondering in the street day and night with nowhere to go! You're homeless! Come on baby, let's do this right!

"Dang girl! You make it hard on a brother with that conversation. You make it sound like I want to accept the crumbs from life's table."

"Well, don't you!"

"Every time you go to prison, you're accepting the crumbs from life's table!" She smacked him on the head! "Gone boy! And another thing! Why didn't you just give them the money and the dope?"

Dino looked at her in hesitation and said, "Baby! I didn't have that much dope or cash; that is the only (emphasizing only) reason we handled the situation in that manner! They wouldn't believe us if we told them we didn't have the money. The streets rule, baby! Whatever it says is law! Let me give you an example! If someone in prison spread gossip you were 'top tier,' they would believe it! Those guys adopted that as true. They got out of prison and tried to rob us. There was absolutely nothing I could do about that. Again I apologize!"

"Apology accepted! Now! Let's go get some breakfast? I know you're hungry! I know I am!" Shawnta said, "Yeah! Sure!" He hugged her real tight, kissed her, and affectionately swayed back and forth.

Word on the street was Dino and Do Good had some involvement in the incident that left two men dead on Wine Hearst Dr. Big Will told his boys in the joint he was going to rob them once he got out of prison; the grapevine in prison also said Do Good got shot and dragged into a vacant house! They knew him as well.

"I think the brothers are in for a surprise; everyone in the street knew the reputation. These brothers would make the barrel on a 9-millimeter melt and the firing pin file out if you rubbed them the wrong way. You better be very careful if you got beef."

On a lighter note, a week after their unfortunate situation, Mike and Jerry called to inform them they'd finally gotten another real estate project and wanted to see if they were still interested. They knew they would be interested considering a part of their parole stipulations said "they must maintain employment or violate parole and return back to prison; HUD agreed to sell them ten houses with the promise not to sell for a period of three years and further only lease to low-income qualified tenants.

They expeditiously agreed to all the terms and conditions in the contract! Now with a total of forty homes in the portfolio and the sixteen-unit complex; money represented power and a strong voice in the community when you played good monopoly and your chess game was up to par. They got on the phone and started dialing numbers, calling every employee on the roster. They were ready to go to work! Darlene collected her crew, and Jonathan collected his. Dino and Do Good were very prompt, ready to work.

Suppressing the kidnapping situation from Mike and Jerry was probably the smartest thing to do because they weren't cut from that kind of cloth! They just wanted an easy ride, not knowing drugs and violence went hand in glove. No matter how much you tried to disassociate one from the other, they seemed to always merge. You couldn't have one without the other! It was implausible! At the first opportunity, Dino asked Mike, "When are we going to get things popping again?"

Mike smiled! He put two fingers up and said, "Two days, G..." That Friday, they took a trip to the resort with the intentions of improvising to make sure no one suspected them of the missing cocaine.

While Mike drove, Jerry reclined his seat and flashed back to Starlet in the pool naked. He couldn't erase that from the blackboards of his mind! It was branded in for life. After a long pause in conversation,

Mike told Jerry, "You know we normally stop by Grandma's house before we do anything!"

Jokingly saying, "So what, man! I'll tell you what, let's stop by Grandma's house anyway because she has the riding gear that we never used at her house!"

Mike was anxious too, thinking this is our opportunity to finally ride together. They both had experience but never enjoyed the fun and laughter of riding together on the trail.

They rushed in to see Grandma and quickly changed into their riding gear, and out the door they went, walking towards the stable, laughing and joking. No one had expected them; you must first call according to protocol to make sure someone's available to accommodate you with a saddle and bridle because horses are different in size, and it might require a larger or smaller apparatus!

Mike said, "Maybe we should get some help!"

Jerry replied, "We don't need a stable hand. My uncle used to own a ranch. I know the correct size to put on a horse."

Mike said, "Okay! Come on!"

Jerry coincidentally went to the opposite end of the stable from where "Stub" was kept in a stall; Stub was the "crazy horse" that hadn't been trained; he wondered why. Without incident, they saddled the horses and raced out of the stable, kicking the horses for speed like an accelerator in a car; they headed straight for the wooded area to get on the horse trail!

Once they made it to the trail, the tempo gradually slowed to a walk. Thirty minutes later, Banks got a phone call from the front gate announcing Bill was at the front gate with the horses. Banks told the gatekeeper to let him in!

He knew 1,500 keys of that powdery white stuff that takes you to another place had just arrived. It was a best friend in some circles and a worst nightmare to others! It could kill you, cripple you for life in the most unthinkable way; the white stuff was unpredictable! Bill smiled and entered the gate, watching as it slowly closed behind him. He drove up the road towards the stable. This was a normal weekly routine! Bill knew exactly where to go. Anytime a shipment came in, the horse trainers would instantly dismiss what they were doing and hurried to unload the truck. That took precedence over any previous job assignments!

As the truck pulled into the stable, Cortez and Bill jumped out. He told him, "Go to the refreshment stand and have them sign the ticket for delivery and enjoy lunch on Pleasure Island Resort." He had absolutely no idea what he was transporting into the facility. Shipments were normally handled by a trucking company that bore the name on its side, "Spring Waters Fountain of Youth," but they occasionally used the horse trailer that was inconspicuous because horses were coming in and out daily!

Cortez took Stub out of his stall. He carefully maneuvered him to the railing and tied him to the post. Usually, Cortez and Martinez were more attentive. If one horse was missing from the stable, they'd know it immediately, but they were missing two horses! It was their duty to report all incidents the minute it occurred.

"I'm sure Mike and Jerry appreciate the negligent oversight!" They certainly didn't want to lose their privileges at Banks Resort. Cortez and Martinez went into the stall, brushed the hay and manure from the trap door that led to an underground storage nest where pounds of cocaine were secreted. It was mandatory to wear safety masks during the moving process to protect against inhaling the strong scent to prevent it from getting into their bloodstream; they would load it into a big basket and lower it down on a hoist. Once it was lowered down, they would climb down the ladder and load it onto an electric-powered cart and transport it to the most amazing hidden compartment transplanted in the wall minutes away from the trap door!

At the very instance Cortez put the last bag in the cart and pulled off in the cart, Mike and Jerry galloped into the stable. They noticed the horse trailer but thought nothing of it at first. They hurried to dismount the horses and get them back into their stalls. After this was done, they curiously walked to the front of the stable where the truck was and couldn't help noticing a horse tied to the pole!

Mike walked towards the horse's stall and saw a trap door leading down into a tunnel; Jerry walked toward the back of the horse trailer, and his eyes popped out of his head while his bottom jaw came unhinged. Excited to discover, Mike called to Jerry, "Come here!"

Jerry ran over to the stall where Mike was to see what he discovered. He thought Mike saw the same thing lying in the stall. It wasn't! Jerry replied, "Dang man, this is a tunnel, but check this out."

They both ran over to the back of the trailer, and Mike saw bags of cocaine lying at the back of the trailer. Apparently, Cortez and Martinez had been drinking on the job again! They left thirty keys of cocaine lying on the tailgate.

Mike said, "This must be where Banks keeps his major supplies." Grabbing two keys, he told Jerry, "Let's get out of here before someone notices we've been here; that way, no one's the wiser. We would be the last two guys suspected of having any connection or involvement with the package being short!"

They cuffed the stuff and ran down the hill, across the golf venue straight to Grandma's condo; now thinking security blanket! Jerry said, "We now have something deep on Banks! If he should find out about us and try to harm us in any kind of way, we can threaten his well-being with the knowledge we have about the drug pipeline hidden underneath the ground."

Mike said, "Well! I'll tell you what we need to do! Go home, get a camera, and sneak back out here to take snapshots of the hidden trap door in the stall." The following week, they returned ready to get some pictures for their portfolio. Surprise! Surprise! Surprise! Stub was loco! Nobody could deal with him but Banks and Cortez.

Jerry said, "Man, how are we going to get in and take pictures? That crazy horse won't let us in." Mike looked around for something useful to brush the straw from the top of the trap door. He saw a push broom lying against the wall and ran over to retrieve it to maneuver the straw. When he put the broom in the stall, at first Stub bucked but calmed down seconds later, giving Mike the opportunity to shuffle the stuff around to see the door. Once accomplished, the camera started flashing. They managed to cover the door without too much interference.

Stub thought they were friendly and not there to harm him. Wiping the nervous sweat from their foreheads as they rapidly exited the stable, they knew the next step was to draw up a letter of extended protection and give it to a family member with the understanding not to publish it unless something terribly tragic happened to them. So they wrote the letter and gave it to Jerry's cousin Sheila with instructions. The envelope was pre-addressed to the New York Daily Tribune!

Chapter 17

Later that Saturday night, Dino and Do Good got a call from Mike. He told them, "I got that good stuff! You guys can work it out any way you want to; just give us what you normally pay. Nothing's changed!"

The next day, Chief Commanding Officer Henderson over "Operation Shutdown" called the honorable Judge Cahill to secure a search and arrest warrant for the arrest of Eugene Phillips residing at 1421 Benson St. for three counts of felony assaults for the willful and malicious intent to cut off the hands of his victims! One count of murder in the second degree for recklessly, with no regard for the law, taking the life of an innocent child strapped in a car safety seat; three counts of destruction of personal property where three vehicles caught on fire and two additional counts of assault charges for the two burned victims caught in the massive fire at the service station. The Judge agreed to the search and arrest of Eugene Phillips!

Henderson went to the court personally to secure the warrants; when he entered the department, he immediately called Officer Brown, Stewart, and two others to go to the home of Eugene Phillips and search the premises for a pouch and a machete, DNA!

Rewind after rewind, the video of Eugene's body structures, both height and weight, appeared to be identical. I know it's a long shot, but we need to pull him in for extensive questioning using the Mutt and Jeff tactic to see if we can shake something internal loose. My gut tells me this is our guy!

Officer Brown and Stewart went to Eugene's mother's home to see if he was there. They went to the address and had no luck there! But luckily, his mom furnished them with a current address, not knowing her son was one of the most wanted terrifying criminals in the State of New York.

When they arrived, knocking on the door, his girlfriend peeked through the hole. Four police officers dressed in black stood at the door; when Erica opened the door, the officers rushed in, snatching him from the couch watching television, threw him to the floor, and applied cuffs.

Brown repeated, "Lay face down on the floor with your hands behind your back!" At first, he resisted! "What am I being arrested for? You have absolutely no right to barge into my home?"

Brown told him that he was a suspect for brutally cutting off three people's hands, burning up a service station, killing an infant, igniting a fire by thrusting a machete down on a man's hand that caused him to lose a limb, and the gas hose cut which disrupted a fire burning three cars and two people.

"We have a warrant for the search of your premises and one for your arrest! I have to inform you that anything you say can and will be used against you in a court of law; you do have an exclusive right to an attorney. If you cannot afford an attorney, the courts will appoint one to represent you!"

He takes another dive for the same offense! The night before, he was at Larry's apartment drinking and smoking blunts!

On a stroke of luck, he slipped through yet another crack. Larry told him, "Relax your machete!" He smiled as he stood up to release his leather pouch that carried his long, gruesome machete. "Hang it in the closet, man!" He continued to unstrap his holster, with DNA absorbed in the fabric. He plopped back down on the couch and continued to drink until it was really late. The alcohol and drugs consumed him.

He told Larry, "I'm going home." So he left the apartment and staggered down the hall to his apartment without his machete! Meanwhile, the search ensued, but nothing turned up, so they ended the search and roughly, very arrogantly, transported him to the station for further interrogation/intimidation! Pulling into the police garage, Eugene had a shrine waiting for him because he had not only startled the entire State of New York, but he had also cut off the hand of one of their fellow officers. They all took a personal interest in the case!

When they brought him through the garage entrance into the department, all officers stopped and stared, with anger and frustration written on their sleeves. They heard the dispatch that the machete bandit had just been arrested, including Officer Collins, who lost his hand to this same lunatic! He was ultimately placed in a cold room with a table and two chairs and a two-way glass for the intended purpose of observation and identification!

Officer Simmons was prohibited from any involvement because he had also lost his hand to the red-light machete bandit; according to departmental policy, if Eugene was the perpetrator responsible for this hideous random act of violence, having Officer Collins involved would only inflame the case and cause bias, prejudice, and an infamous miscarriage of justice!

However, he too knew from dispatch that the red-light machete bandit had been caught and just walked into the department. At this point, he really didn't give a damn about departmental policy. He had to meet this guy face to face so he could show him the damage he caused in his life. He robbed him of full use of his hand and deprived him of the opportunity to work outside the department. Finally, after an hour of sitting in a quiet room alone, he retrospectively thought about what type of evidence they could possibly have against him.

"Could there be a possible eyewitness to either of the crimes?" He knew he hadn't made any mistakes out in the field, so he decided not to say anything to avoid incriminating himself.

An officer came in and spun the chair around to sit on it, with the back of the chair facing Eugene. He began to explain the severity of the accusations against him in hopes of getting him to fall on his sword in exchange for a plea agreement.

He told Eugene, "We have overwhelming circumstantial evidence that could put you away for life! We have video footage that displays the person of interest running away from the scene of the crime with one arm and the exact size and weight you have."

Eugene replied, "Man, you just racial profiled me because I have one arm. Do you realize how many people have one arm? Do you know there are tons of people with the same weight and height with one arm? Come on! You can't charge me with that crime!"

The officer knew he wasn't bulging, so he tried another method to get him to confess. The bandit was solid! He refused to be outmaneuvered by some lame cop!

Two more officers came in to interrogate him, pushing and shoving him around the room; soon they left to regroup because they were getting nowhere.

"Look who's coming down the hall straight to the interrogation room!" Collins and his partner were plotting how he would go in while Officer James posted outside the door to stop him from beating this guy if the wrong person happened to come down the hall!

He entered the door and just stood there, staring in silence at the red-light machete bandit, flashing back to when he lost his hand. The more he continued to remain in that state, the angrier he became! He blurted out, "You are clueless! You don't even know who I am! Do you?" Slowly rolling his right sleeve up to reveal the ugly scar wrapped around his wrist.

Instantly, he went into a rage, grabbing the red-light machete bandit and throwing him into the wall. He clinched him again, panting vigorously as they both stumbled to the floor, with Officer Collins toppling over him! At this time, Commander Henderson was walking towards the interrogation room to get one last crack at him before he was booked.

Officer James noticed him and rushed in to get Collins out of there quickly before he was caught. They both exited the area without attracting any attention. Henderson walked in and calmly sat down to question Eugene.

"Looks like you've been in a scuffle! You've got a bruise on your eye!" Eugene thought he was just trying to be funny. He probably sent those guys in to rough him up so he could cave in. So he responded, "You got jokes! Ha! Ha! I think you should try writing better material; do you see why the department needs an overhaul, rehabilitation?"

Henderson told him he understood how someone could be easily misunderstood and treated so badly to the point where their anger was misplaced and channeled the wrong way. "I understand your frustration as a youngster and how you could have been a victim of bullying and held it in so long you wound up attempting to cause unthinkable harm to yourself through suicidal attempts such as the one exercised here. My bottom line is, I really want to help you, but in order for me to do so, you must first help me help you! I understand you may not want to talk now, but if you have a change of heart, just ask for me. Oh! You do understand you are facing a possible life sentence if you decide to go to trial. Food for thought, son!"

Chapter 18

The entire state was looking for an end to this tragic story, and those jurors all had zero tolerance for this type of behavior. Four hours later, they booked and fingerprinted him and threw him in a holdover cell to be transported to the county jail, where he would be detained pending an arraignment by the court to assess his bond, read the pending charges, and explain to him that he had a guaranteed right under the law to have a court-appointed attorney represent him if he could not afford to retain one!

Eugene had been arrested again, but it looked like this time they were going to keep him for a while. Three days later, he was on the docket to appear in court! Judge Cahill read his charges and asked him how he pleaded; he replied, "Not guilty."

The bailiff escorted him out of the court and put him in a small room 10' by 4' wide with two benches the length of the room! Twenty minutes later, a turnkey came to the door and opened it; in walked this very attractive attorney with her associate staying close by. He extended his hand to make her acquaintance!

She assumed the lead! "My name is Ms. Alexis Crammer, and this is Attorney John Wilkerson, an intern with the court doing field research studies. The court appointed me as your attorney to represent you on the allegations pending against you! Is there anything you would like to share with me, Eugene?"

He was witty! "All I can tell you is I'm not responsible for these crimes. I may resemble the guy, but that doesn't mean I'm the guy.

No one has positively identified me as the perpetrator! It has been said if a white man catches a cold, a black man catches pneumonia. I can't believe this is happening. The grand jury will indict a glass of contaminated water. I know they're going to indict me."

Crammer replied, "I'm sorry for your lack of trust in the judicial system, as well as your unfortunate situation that got you here, but what we're going to do is file the appropriate motions for discovery and disclosure to have them turned over to us every piece of evidence they have against you that remotely insinuates you are the alleged perpetrator! Now listen! I want you to know it's going to be a waiting game if you can't post bail, but I promise those motions will be in court within the week, Eugene! Thanks! Alexis: I'll be in touch with you as the case develops! Here's my card! If you find out something or something comes to mind that may be conducive to your case, please don't hesitate to give me a call."

Eugene was 26 years old and ran faster than Ben Johnson on his worst day! I had to tell you the cops were extremely lucky to catch this guy before he could get on his feet; boy, were they lucky! Eugene contemplated, "How long am I going to be here?" Going back to lock-up after the interview with his attorney, it was lunchtime.

Trays were passed through an open shuttle to the inmates one at a time! Suddenly, from nowhere, a voice from the back of the cell block yelled out, "Little John, don't touch none of those trays; your tray is mine!" Scared to death, he backed away from the porthole where they issued the trays and sat down on a stationary stool attached to the bars, with his head down in a depressed kind of way. He, along with several other first-timers, was extorted, sexually abused, and made to wash other inmates' clothes on the tier! It seemed like those guys were scientists who'd been in and out of the system; they actually knew when someone was afraid, and they capitalized on their vulnerabilities!

There was no pity or sympathy for anyone in the system. You were exclusively on your own to defend against whatever came your way. Going inside was the ultimate, the most deadly slippery slope you'd probably ever encounter in your absolute wildest uncanny dream! "Prisons are none other than schools for thieves!" Did you think he was going to get better or worse? One thing for certain, it was definitely going to be a challenge!

Speaking of a challenge, Starlet Templeton requested a meeting time with Robert to discuss another idea to resolve the ongoing problem with large amounts of cocaine evaporating into thin air! Walking into her office, Robert smiled and acknowledged her profound beauty in a very professional way. "So, you think you've found a definite solution to our problem?" he asked.

Starlet replied, "Yes! What we can do is refresh all of the smoke detectors in all units! This is the season. The only twist is we will secretly install a unit next to Ms. Reid and her units as well, equipped with hidden cameras in the rooms that have visual and/or physical connection with the hidden compartments in the china cabinet! Now, I know it's quite illegal, but who gives a damn? Let's bring this ordeal to a close!"

Banks said, "Good idea, Starlet! I'll get it mandated immediately and have Jack do the installation as soon as tomorrow." Banks pulled his cell from his holster and called Jack to explain in detail his project for tomorrow.

Jack replied, "Of course! I'll get on it first thing in the morning. It's a bit late now to start the installations; we don't want to impose!"

"Okay! Well, that's settled! I can't wait to catch these guys. I don't understand why they haven't considered an itinerary kept at the front gate that might help. How unscrupulous!"

Sitting at home, watching the football game and listening to their police scanner to stay current on the flow of the streets, if the police plotted a raid, they would know which direction they were coming from, leaving them a venue to make their quick, delusional departure! Laid back, enjoying freedom, the ladies were getting snacks for the game and drinking CODIVA with a premier mix, choking on a joint like Miley Cyrus, Snoop, and Michael Phelps with his turbo lungs!

Dino and his brother had become the talk of the hood! Dino was 29, and Do Good was 28 years old, hustling the streets legally by day and prowling like unlicensed traveling salesmen by night, moving cocaine north, east, south, and west, grinding hard!

They were determined to work hard on both sides of the equation to make ends meet because someday soon it would be their time to buy some real estate and turn their negative into a positive; that was provided Do Good discontinued his extravagant spending habits! He spent most of his earnings on the women in the streets.

He had absolutely too many women he was trying to take care of; unless they put something in the pot, they weren't doing anything but leaning on him for his chatter.

When he wasn't with Dino or his main lady Tabitha, he would be in the streets surrounded by cute women, in the clubs, or turning corners trying to get paid. Dino got a text! "I got to see who this is trying to help me pay this light bill! Hello, who's this?"

"Hey man, this is Lumpy! I need two O's!"

Dino replied, "I got you! Meet me at the gas station on Brookshire!" When Lumpy arrived, Dino was pumping gas. Lumpy parked his car on the sideline, jumped in with Dino, and they drove through the car wash, where the transaction went down. The noise pollution prevented the narcotics drug task force from picking up on the dialogue. Before Dino made it back from the drop-off, Do Good picked up two calls, one guy requesting an ounce and the other wanted two!

He thought he'd go and knock that out before Dino got back. He told both of them to meet him in Kentucky Fried Chicken. When he saw them walk in, he got up from the booth where he sat drinking a cup of coffee and navigated toward the restroom! Blue and "Q" were regular customers, slamming twice a week.

Do Good made it back to the spot before his brother, pulling in one behind the other.

"Do Good, I see you got more beer!"

Dino replied, "Yeah, dirty! You know I had to pick up some of that!"

The next day, Dino rolled out, trying to find something to get into. He stopped very briefly at the club to get a drink and bounce. When he left the club a little tipsy, failing to yield at a stop sign and failing to use his signature light changing lanes, the police pulled him over to learn he was wanted for questioning in a double homicide on Larry Harper (AKA Big Will) and Corky Robinson (AKA Suicide)!

Once they arrived at the station, he was told, "We can make this easy or hard!" Dino knew there was no easy nothing in a homicide.

"What do you mean I can make it easy or hard? I don't understand what you're talking about. Abreast me!"

Officer Spencer said, "You know damn well what we're talking about. Murder!"

Spencer paused for a minute! Sometimes silence is worth its weight in gold. Detective Lynch always played the bad cop because he was tailor-made for it. "Listen, young punk! You are on parole for robbery. You went back on a parole violation and a new charge for carrying a concealed weapon! Prior to that, you had problems as a child. You know I remember you. I've arrested you many times. But listen! You have finally met the big boys! You have been implicated in a double homicide."

Dino replied, "With all due respect, I don't have a clue what you're talking about. You're wasting your time questioning me. I don't have beef with nobody. I would appreciate it if you would go ahead and wrap this conversation up if you're not going to charge me because I don't know anything about it."

Officer Spencer said, "Dino, now just calm down. Here! Would you like to have a cigarette?"

"No sir! I don't smoke! You can't con me with that guy bad guy bull."

Detective Lynch said, "Dino, we're not trying to bull you around. There are entirely too many things a lot more interesting we could be doing besides playing a game with you! Alright, I'll tell you what! Let's cut through all the bull that you mentioned and get right down to it. Your prints were on the steering wheel of the car that the murdered victim was driving."

Dino explained, "I knew both of them from the joint, and they promised when they got out they would stop by and let me see how they were doing. So when they came home, Big Will asked me if I wanted to test drive his car; of course, I said yeah. I drove it around the block a few days ago; that's how my prints came about. I didn't know they'd gotten killed; they just came home about two weeks ago."

The boy deserved a scholarship in charisma! He baffled the two officers holding dismayed poker hands. The officers put him in a cell while they decided what they wanted to do. Clearly, they didn't have anything concrete worthy of a trial by a jury. Dino paced back and forth, turning thoughts over in his head. "I'm glad I took the gun and dumped it. I thought I wiped my fingerprints from the steering wheel. I only hope Shawnta didn't touch anything in the back seat that would come to haunt us; they would have mentioned if her prints were on something! Maybe they can't compare her print because she's never been arrested before!"

Thoughts were running all over the place, but he knew at the end of the day his silence was truly his best friend. Thinking again! "Could they hold me pending an investigation? Can my parole officer detain me?" He cluttered in thought until a prisoner down the hall yelled, "Who's that just came in? What'd they get you for? Send me a cigarette!"

Dino replied, "I don't smoke!"

"Dang!" said the prisoner!

The two officers spoke with the chief, who said, "Under the circumstances, there's not quite enough evidence to detain Mr. Henson. We have to let him go and follow his bread trails to get more evidence against him!"

Dino was in the back of the cell using the urinal when the guard yelled, "Harvey Henson, come on out; you're being released." Dino ran to the front of the cell, impatiently waiting for the guard to open the door. He went down the elevator with a guard escort, stopping at the desk to get his personal belongings. He got back on the elevator to go down to the first floor. Once he got off, he went straight to the vending machine to get cigarettes, a soda, and called Do Good to come pick him up from the county jail!

"Do Good," he said, "man, I was waiting on your call. What happened?"

"They just let me go. I'll tell you when you get here."

He was there in 20 minutes flat! He pulled in front of the building with his flashers on. Dino saw him pull up and walked out of the jail.

It was slushy, so Dino hit his heels on the frame of the car before he got in.

"Do Good," he asked, "man, what happened? How did you get pulled over?"

Dino explained, "They initially stopped me because I failed to yield at a stop sign and didn't use my signal light when changing lanes."

"Man, that's bull crap!" Do Good exclaimed.

"But wait a minute! Once they got me in custody, they told me that I was wanted for questioning for the murder of Corky Robinson and Larry Harper. They said my fingerprints were on the steering wheel. I told those fools they stopped by a few days before they got killed and let me drive their new whip. That's how my prints got on the steering wheel. They bought it! I know they probably have me under investigation, and I have to be really careful not to make any wrong moves."

"They don't have anything because they don't have an eyewitness! Don't sweat it!" Do Good reassured him.

"I hope the parole officer doesn't call me in for it."

"In New York, Manhattan? Who doesn't get pulled over for questioning! She'll probably tell you not to worry as long as nothing else comes up that warrants an arrest. Man, we are all suspects in this city!"

The minute Dino walked through the door, his mom stopped him in his tracks. "Boy, what happened to you? Why are the police picking you up again?"

"Momma, I got picked up because they wanted to ask questions about a double homicide that happened around the corner! My guess is because I grew up in the hood with a criminal history. I know everything and everybody."

She said, "I'm glad that's all they wanted. You weren't involved in that mess, were you?"

"No, momma! That's not my bag! It would be totally out of character for me to do something inhumane like that!"

Ms. Henson replied, "They had me really worried; I didn't know what to think. No matter how old you get, you are still my baby. I love you!" A tear fell from her eye.

Two weeks before Dino was taken in for questioning, he met a young lady named Ebony Crawford; she was twenty-two years old, with one kid named Dominic! She lived in a rundown apartment with one bedroom, a kitchen, a bath, and a living room owned by Mr. Jordan, a slumlord (AKA King of the Slum Lords). Ebony had just completed her required drug rehabilitation program! He couldn't tell by her incredible, vivacious appearance! He looked at her as another struggling sister down on her luck.

She received welfare benefits, was in the Section Eight housing program, and was a recipient of Social Security because her baby daddy got killed in military combat! He was really attracted to her;

she had a street-savvy intuition that was on point. She would do anything for Do Good.

Chapter 19

Eventually, she convinced him to let her help him move his packages with her seductive persuasion and intriguingly eloquent enunciation. She was determined to try extra hard to win him over because she knew he had other ladies in his life, and she certainly didn't want to be listed in a low-ranking category! She didn't want to see him only in the interim when things weren't going well with his other ladies; Ebony wanted a strong, independent brother with a rough edge who knew how to make things manifest!

Not someone she could easily control and maneuver like a puppet on a string or a priceless chess piece; that was a turn-off. It only made her level of interest depreciate, and her respect diminished rapidly. They were talking about successful, crafty businessmen, not wimps.

"A weak man is only worth a one-night experience," she thought. Do Good was exactly what she wanted in a man; his face should have been printed on the one-thousand-dollar bill because he wore it well! Do Good persuaded his brother to put her in the mix. "We need another horse; why not? She was oriented! She started out with a small package to give her an opportunity to build a clientele. Ebony knew she wasn't ready for this just getting out of rehab.

It was her trigger! She knew it too! The drug enticed her back for more, and she fell for it. Back in the rotation! Excited! Her first package was one ounce, rocked up as a test. They sent her to the store to get baking soda and a "swisher"! That was a cigar! They would rock and measure it all in eight balls (rolling)! Dino said, "I have one thing to say! Don't ever undress this bitch."

They supplied her and sent her out on the field to handle her business. Ebony's take was seven hundred, and the brothers got fourteen hundred off each ounce sold. For a while, everything went well until one day Do Good came in unexpectedly and caught her in bed, wearing only her panties and choking on that glass pipe. He was stunned! It felt like a dagger plunged into his chest! His mind didn't want his eyes to believe what they'd seen. He was just beginning to anticipate changing some things around in his lifestyle for her; another Cinderella story turned sour!

He ran in the room, snatched the pipe from her, and threw it against the wall, kneeling on his knees, hugging her as she cried in disappointment. "Do Good, what are you doing? You promised you were finished with that stuff."

Ebony replied, "Baby, I relapsed; what can I say? You just threw the smoking gun against the wall! I offer no excuse other than I'm weak to the drug, and I'm sorry; you have the right to put your hands on me like that!"

"Do Good," he said, "we have to get you back on top; we cannot move forward with this kind of baggage!"

Ebony said, "I know! What can I do to conquer this suicidal drug?"

"First, you have to learn all over again how to love yourself! If you love yourself, it won't allow you to engage or indulge in things destructive to your health or well-being. Look at me! Here I am, telling you how to better yourself when I should be listening to my own advice! All I can say is you're in a very toxic place, and it doesn't get better unless you want it."

Ebony replied, "You are absolutely right, baby! I'm done! I'm going to get this paper and stay focused on my family, having a better life. The teaspoon of wisdom you supplied me with is worth its weight in gold. That's all the encouragement I need to jolt me back on track so I can take another serious look at myself through the windows of reality, to envision my potentially disastrous future staring me directly in the eye! Do Good, I love you for that…"

"Do Good replied, "Now can I get my counseling session fee?"

She smiled! He started undressing and climbed in the bed with her. "Um! You taste so good. What's your recipe?"

"Ebony said, "Boy, you're so silly," pulling him closer!

Thirty minutes later, the phone rang. "Ring! Ring!" Ebony answered the phone after glancing at the caller ID. "Hey Dino, what's up? Let me speak with my brother!"

"Okay, hold on! Here! It's your brother!"

"Hey, playa, what's going on?"

"Dino said, "I need you to make a run with me; I got a big fish on the line, and I don't want to be out there in the water by myself."

"No problem! Give me 20 minutes… I got you, man!"

They met with the guys and sold five ounces. Right after that was taken care of, he went back to Ebony's apartment to further encourage her to go back through treatment because she obviously missed some of the rudiments in the process!

Do Good had a huge appetite for the ladies, but he took a special interest in her; she had an aura that attracted like suction powerful enough to pull the air out of the Grand Canyon! "She's fine!" he thought. He had an objective. He wanted to get paid, and having that persona along was malpractice! He knew the rules of the game, and that was a definite no!

Ebony was admitted back into drug treatment so she could walk through the steps again! Education teaches that if you don't get it right the first time, you'll have to revisit it; that's real life, no fronting! She was really proud of Do Good. Despite the fact he dealt drugs and was off the chain with other women, he showed a compassion, a love no other man had ever shown. He genuinely gave her the very best advice he could possibly give and took her by the hand back to treatment and registered.

Do Good called her mother after she was admitted. She told him, "This is the second time she's been admitted into treatment!"

"Do Good was a little surprised."

She continued, "The first time she went in for treatment, she was just 21 years old, modeling for Playboy."

"One day, she was in her room at the Playboy Mansion doing what was customary for her. A news editor happened to innocently open the door, and in walks Hefner, who proceeded to escort them in, telling his successful life story embellished with the incredible living arrangement he has. Unfortunately, he stumbled into Ebony's room and witnessed her totally relaxed, caught smoking crack cocaine! To prevent the bad press and publicity, Ebony had to undergo drug treatment to cure her chemical dependency; she never went back to the mansion!"

"Do Good said, 'I am so sorry to hear that, Ms. Crawford. But I'll tell you what! I'm going to do everything I can to help her get her life back on track. She truly deserves better. Thanks for sharing that intimate information with me about your daughter.'"

On the other side of the equation, Mike and Jerry were preparing for Dino and Do Good's "remake." They had just unloaded two keys and planned to return to the scene of the crime that same weekend to pick up another key; only this time, the camera told no lies. Caught with the smoking gun! This was where the proverbial snowball intensified with excessive coercion as it continued to roll into a dark, scary, unsubtle place of uncertainty. The youngsters were about to step into a world where everyone wore masks!

Chapter 20

Everyone was a stranger, like two ships passing in the night without a signal light to broadcast at least a silhouette—not even a clue a ship was coming! Guards held incredibly high in defense mode; everybody was a suspect!

Mike and Jerry's eerie plan to go back to the resort to pick up another package wasn't quite smart; they obviously knew the pipeline wasn't going to last forever. Banks was no fool! Boy, was their intuition telling them right! They were caught on camera! Starlet knew Robert would jump through the roof to find out this exciting news. Unfortunately, he was out of town on business and wasn't due back until the following week. Starlet couldn't wait to break the urgent news.

She first tried calling his cell, but the lines were down. She immediately followed up by calling his secretary to see if she could get him on the line, to no avail. "Have him contact me ASAP," she told her, "the second he walks into his office. It is urgent that I speak with him concerning Ms. Reid's condo situation finally resolved."

When he returned, his secretary informed him that the bookkeeper, Ms. Templeton, expressed a dire need to speak with him. He assumed unambiguously that she had trapped the perpetrators who had been taking his merchandise. Without hesitation, he called her into his office.

She walked in with her laptop. "You're not going to believe what you're about to witness, so hold your breath." Turning on her computer, she politely spun it around to face Banks, revealing Mike dismounting the switch cover plate from the wall, activating the inside switch to open the cabinet, and then removing a key of cocaine.

"Grandma has absolutely no knowledge that scandalous little punks had the audacity to rob me!" He was in awe! He couldn't believe what he had just witnessed right before his very eyes, thinking audibly, "What am I going to do about this mess? To think I've really grown to like those kids, but something has to be done." He had time to think about the consequences because it wouldn't be another week before they returned!

Now he understood why the kids didn't get entrapped by "Operation Safe Mode." When they were terminated from their jobs, the machine wasn't applicable to them. That lifted a huge burden from his shoulders to know Eckert and others weren't in any way a part of this insidiously elaborate scheme to steal drugs from him! It was ingenious for them to have gotten away with eight keys in that period of time without getting caught, but they had to pay the piper.

He called his boys, Jack Eckert, and four other co-owners into his office to decide what to do with Mike and Jerry; everybody instantly decided elimination was the only answer! They knew entirely too much! Starlet interrupted, flashing back to the pool! Of course, she had a hidden agenda to rescue Dino; she was deeply infatuated with his swagger!

"Robert," she said, "I think they would be very useful! It's not like they betrayed your trust as a friend or employee, but quite the contrary: two complete strangers out to make a hustle like you. Now that they know who you are and what you really do for a living, you can program them to think the way you want them to. I really think they'll be an asset. As you can see, they are ambitious and have a unique style that can't be denied. It's your decision! I thought there may be something you might want to consider to avoid resulting in a more drastic measure!"

That following Friday, before they arrived, Mr. Banks instructed the guard at the front gate to have them come to his office; he had an electrical power surge in the basement and needed their assistance to help troubleshoot the equation. Pulling into the entrance, the guard followed his orders. "Mr. Banks assumed you guys may be coming in today, so he asked me to have you come to his office."

"I think he wants you to repair something for him," they both replied. "Sure thing!" Once they arrived, Banks told them, "I want to show you the ongoing problems we're having in one of the older units."

Going down a flight of stairs to the basement area, they proceeded to travel by an electric-powered cart. Suddenly, four men with automatic weapons appeared as they turned the corner! "Oh my God!" They knew Banks had figured it out. A suspenseful moment came over them, not knowing what the repercussions might be.

One of the men instructed them to sit down! The other men began tying them to a chair. Banks remained amazingly quiet, calm, and in control. In a somber tone of voice, he asked, "Why did you steal from me?" Everything went silent!

Dropping their heads in prayer was the only possible recourse available; laryngitis kicked in, and their voice boxes denied access. At that point, the two guards began beating them for nearly fifteen minutes, leaving them nearly unconscious! Both of them trembled, feeling fright and helpless; they had never seen this side of Mr. Banks! He was "cruel and unusual" and had absolutely no compassion for what they had done to him.

Remaining calm, they still assumed they had the upper hand with the incriminating pictures of the horse stall and cocaine. "You guys have taken over eight keys from me, and you have to repay me at street value with a 50% hike in interest rate! Here are your stipulations you must follow to the letter; otherwise, the penalty is death by means unimaginable to mankind.

From this point forward, you guys are "mules," packers responsible for importing and exporting goods! Picking up and dropping off money, drugs, and weapons. You are commanded to either commit or take part in committing murders and arsons on call to destroy evidence and eliminate government witnesses or someone who has maliciously betrayed the trust of the Cartel! Make it clear you must continue dropping off the loads you were unloading on Dino and Do Good, with a smaller percentage for themselves, barring only living expenses to carry them from month to month, with perks every so often!

Chapter 21

Mike and Jerry weren't as lucky as Meshach, Shadrach, and Abednego. Under drastic enormous mounting pressure, the course of their destinies changed. They were no longer allowed to navigate their ship; Banks had seized total control over them, and he had absolutely no regard for the safety or precarious situations that might unfold!

"Payback!" Mike said. "You can't compel us to commit random acts of violence at your command!"

"We refuse to let you antagonize us with this bull crap you're attempting to pull. I have never been one to submit to a man out of fear. Besides, I have as much right to be upset as you for insidiously secreting drugs in my grandmother's home, putting her in harm's way for any of a thousand things that can possibly happen as a consequence of having something in there she knew absolutely nothing about. You used to be my mentor! With that said, I am willing to repay you if you'll let us just work it out, but that interest stuff you're talking about, you can keep that. You don't deserve the interest; grandma deserves the interest!"

It got worse for Mike and Jerry! The more he talked, the worse it got! He didn't know when to put the shovel down. His adrenaline started rising. He thought he'd convinced him. Mike continued, "You're lucky we didn't go to the cops when we first discovered drugs hidden in the china cabinet."

Banks absorbed all the information, not uttering a word. Mike said, "I think it's only fair to inform you we not only know your stash is hidden in the cabinet but underneath the horse's stall as well. We have pictures and documented proof of money laundering and much more. We even have letters tucked away ready to be mailed to the Daily Tribune, the news media, the United States, and the State of New York's Attorney General if anything should happen to us. If we so much as sprain an ankle, you better fix it."

Banks looked over at his entourage, and one of the guys came from behind Dino and stomped his ankle hard!

"Banks said, 'I guess that means we're in trouble.'" He appeared unshaken by the idle threats. He told his bodyguards, "Untie both of them." They escorted them to another sub-level basement beneath the basement; it must have been an emergency shelter from tornadoes and hurricanes. Entering this room, they saw operating tables, hospital beds, hangover lights, cabinets filled with instruments used to perform surgeries, with doctors and nurses on staff to assist in actual surgeries!

Jerry grew nervous, trying to get Mike's attention through his body language to share the terror through his eyes; neither knew what to think about the subliminal suspense: "Why are we in a hospital?" Everything happened so quickly.

The guards thrust them onto operating tables, strapping them down like they were Frankenstein! Seconds later, a doctor entered with a needle; that was all they remembered! They were convinced the incriminating evidence leveraged against them had worked. He gave them an anesthetic that put them under for an hour. When they awakened, Banks was standing over them, smiling.

He said to them both, "Gentlemen, you have just awakened from an anesthetic used to put you under for one hour; in that time period, we implanted a model device extraordinarily designed to notice there's a visible scar just above your left hip area—that's where the device is located. Now! What I would like to share with you is the diabolical method used to compel the abeyance of my every command. What you have inside you is an incredibly sensitive monitor with three features that enslaves you for life! You must always remember those three things:

The device has a built-in recorder that transmits everything you say.

It has a built-in GPS with unlimited capabilities!

The most famously attractive feature is the laser with lightning-fast aggression that will kill faster than the speed of light.

So you see, fellows, we have your balls in the palm of our hands! This hand-held device called a transmitter is the instrument used to instantly destroy every vital organ in your body, starting with the most important, your pancreas, which is where it has been implanted. Unfortunately, your lives are open books, and the cameras are on 24/7. You're under constant watch to prevent any possible manipulation of the sensitive device!"

Mike and Jerry had met their wits' end, exasperated with contemplation of how to overcome this horrible nightmare they had walked into like a dream with one distinction: you can't walk out once you're in. They knew it was to their advantage to honor all requests tendered by Banks at least until they could figure something out.

One thing was clear; they had to find out where the transmitter was secretly kept and how to elude him; until this was achieved, careful communication was an important concern. Knowing someone could be listening in to their conversations any time, day or night!

Sign language and texting was the only communication they could resort to, short of writing notes!

"Jerry," Mike asked, "Mr. Banks, what do you want us to do?"

"Banks replied, 'Well, for starters, I want you to bring me two hundred thousand dollars of that money you have hidden. Then we'll go from there. I will set up distribution arrangements. This wasn't meant to happen this way, but you fell into it because you had guts and sticky fingers!'"

"Mike said, 'You don't expect us back on Sunday, do you?'"

"No! I'll see you guys on Monday evening after work!"

Banks ordered them released from restraints. He was confident he could relax his leash without fear of betrayal. He had exclusive dominion over whether they lived or died at the press of a button; they were his puppets!

As they nervously walked across the parking lot like little kids in grade school, Mike began sobbing in fear as though he had just entered the gates of hell! A pitch-dark tunnel with not a sign of light; a spooky place of uncertainty where wits were considered obsolete. In the same breath, Mike uttered with enthusiasm, "There's got to be a way out!"

"Jerry, I told you I had bad vibes the last time. My gut told me something was wrong; back off! I never thought in a million years we would get caught stealing from a drug cartel; being connected to a device that translates everything we do, everything we say; and thrust under dictatorship to follow any order presented to us for execution.

"Jerry! We knew messing with that deadly drug meant you'd die one way or the other. Either you're killed by someone or commit suicide through the usage of a drug you thought you knew very well! You didn't have a clue. Here we are, successful entrepreneurs with over thirty pieces of real estate, trapped in the spider's web all because of greed. A thoughtless irresistible temptation that could have easily been avoided!"

Jerry opened the glove box to grab a pen and paper and began to write the words, "Where there's a will, there's a way. We have to get that device out of his possession. Until then, let's just play his game. The bright side, no matter what we do, is we have a very good explanation. We'll find a way." They both looked at one another and smiled. They were in for the challenge; giving up wasn't an option!

An educated guess would be to do the right thing for a while in the hope he'd drop his guard. "But Mike! What are we going to tell Carol and Sherry? You know it won't be long before they put the puzzle together: you have a slit in your pancreas area, and so do I. Sherry's going to notice my scar as soon as I enter the door with her little freaky self!"

Chapter 22

Mike pulled onto the service station lot and texted Jerry. He explained to him that they were going to tell them the truth so that they would know how to communicate to avoid saying the wrong thing. "Further, if we put our heads together and carefully plan, we can counteract and defuse his strategy."

Jerry shook his head, indicating "Yes!" "That sign language course would be useful now!" Once they arrived home, still badly shaken, Mike went in with Jerry to help explain what had happened and to comfort Sherry, to make sure she didn't fall to pieces.

Jerry stuck his key in the door, checking to make sure she was properly dressed before he gave Mike the okay to come in. Sherry walked out of the kitchen into the living room, bare feet and inquisitive. "Where will your disappearance all day take me if I was psychic? Tell the truth!"

"Jerry: Baby, we were robbed! I don't want to talk about it right now! I'll explain it to you later." At the same time, he put his finger to his mouth, non-verbally telling her to be quiet. He quickly got his cell phone from its holster and hurried to text her to explain what had really happened.

While Jerry explained, Mike pulled his shirt up to reveal the incision! On the text, he frantically wrote, "Mike and I are monitored." Mike had already shown her his scar; now Jerry pulled up his shirt to unveil his scar! He went on to explain what had happened and the dangers involved with the device implanted inside them. She was hysterical, knowing that all of their lives were in potentially grave danger.

Mike asked her to calm down after placing his hand over her mouth. He told her how difficult it would be for the two of them to explain it to Carol, so "you have to call her and give her the bad news! We'll have to figure out different ways of communication to circumvent them from knowing what we have on the table."

Sherry nodded her head with calmness and gave a thumbs-up. She texted Jerry to tell him, "I love you, and we're going to get through this together!"

Mike smiled and walked out the door to get home so he could explain how they planned a possible strategy to secure the device.

Carol was waiting for him at the door. Before he could turn the key, Carol opened the door wide, hugged him, and kissed him like he had terminal cancer, with one day to live and was on the way home from the hospital!

"Carol: That dirty son of a ----! I could kill him; he has taken complete control over our lives, compelling you and Jerry to do his dirty work and invade your privacy! That's an intrusion into the intimate personal space. He certainly has his nerve! We can't have a sexual moment without this guy throwing some pass interference eavesdropping. All he needs now is a big screen TV…Damn, Mike! What are we going to do?"

"Mikes replied, 'We can't let him get the best of us! We'll find a way. He'll slip! There must be a doctor skillful enough to remove it without annoyance!'"

Mike got a pen and paper and started writing! "Jerry and I have to deliver to him. We have to give him two hundred thousand dollars on Monday after work. At that point, he'll tell us what he wants our next mission." He put the pen down and asked, "What does the lady of the house have in mind for dinner?"

"Carol: I was thinking steak and rice with a salad and peach cobbler for dessert; how does that sound?"

"Mike: That's what I've been craving! Are you a mind reader or something?"

"Carol: You'll never know!"

"Mike: Plus we can go to the movies to check out the new release 'Flash.'"

Carol turned up the stereo intentionally to create distortion. On Monday, they also had to see Dino and Do Good to pick up and drop off another key. They had to make sure their rehab crew would be there on time; they had a full plate on Monday.

Miles away, Banks sat at the office with his feet resting on his desk, thinking! A jolted thought suddenly suggested he call Samantha. He picked up the receiver, punched in numbers, and rang, rang, rang. Samantha's secretary answered the phone.

"How may I direct your call?"

"This is Mr. Banks. How are you doing? I would like to speak with Ms. Templeton."

"Can you hold for a sec?"

"Banks: Yeah, sure!"

"Samantha: Robert! How's my man doing? Everything's good here. I was just about to walk out to lunch. Call me back on my cell."

"Okay," said Banks. Her cell phone rang, and she picked up on the first ring. "Yeah!" She was walking out of her office, pulling the door shut behind her.

"Conversation continues! What's going on?"

"Robert responded, 'We have finally caught the two guys that were stealing packages of cocaine. It turned out the kids, Mike and Jerry, who I hired nearly a year ago. I've grown to really like them, but under the circumstances, them knowing too much, I had no other alternative but to install our control device in the interior walls of their bodies. You know the penalty when someone betrays or oversteps certain boundaries in the organization!'"

While she was taking lunch, her secretary went into her office to get a fax. Noisy! She glanced at Samantha's desk and couldn't help but notice her black ledger and itinerary lying on the desk. She had to be grossly distracted to leave unsecured privileged client information exposed like this.

She started reading names! "Tiger, Usher, Brad Pitt, Shaquille O'Neal, Michael Jordan, Kobe Bryant, Dennis Rodman, Clinton, David Letterman, Tony Parker, Brett Favre, Brad Pitt, Usher, Snoop Dogg, Will Smith, Reggie Bush, T.I., Ice Cube, Ice-T, Britney Spears, Christina Aguilera, Jessie James, Laurence Fishburne, Charlie Sheen, who used to get his action from Heidi's girl, 'P Diddy Bad Boy,' Jamie Foxx, 50 Cent, Robert Downey Jr., and Ellen DeGeneres."

The ledger read a net profit of 50 million for the year 2024! The secretary was aroused, scanning the "A List." The client list was amazing, with lots of prominent entertainers, ballplayers, and the like. Banks had underground tunnels just like Diddy, without the freak parties—only business. They frequented the business and often bumped into one another to make appointments to spend time with the girls.

"What comes in Samantha's place stays in Samantha's place, like Sin City; they even used the girls in videos and movies as dancers and stunt doubles!"

She and Robert talked for an hour. Banks was overjoyed on one hand, while Mike and Jerry were going in circles, trying to catch their tails.

"Carol told Mike, 'I'm going to Mom's house to get a recipe; I'll be right back.' She was delirious, coupled with enormous amounts lifted off her shoulders; her chest tightened from the pressure with severe signs of a heart attack! Experiencing a slight stumble as she cleared the step onto the porch, she rang the bell as she gasped for breath!

Her mother opened the door to witness Carol in a scary, delusional, and disoriented state with fear written all over her; she clutched her for support and slowly walked her into the house.

Down to her knees she went, with her mom holding her as she assisted in her breaking fall to the floor! Kneeling in prayer with repentance, she asked God to remove all demons from their path and walk them down the path of righteousness. Her mom continued to hold her like she was a little baby, rocking back and forth, telling her, "It's going to be alright. Whatever you've done, he will forgive you for all your sins. He is the gatekeeper capable of putting a shield around you that cannot be penetrated!

"Tell Momma what happened?"

She sniffed, holding onto her mom as she skittishly explained the horrifying situation Mike and Jerry had gotten all of them involved in.

"Ms. Pruitt: There's got to be a way to overcome this. We just have to remain humble and patient, and it will work itself out. Remember, grief is stern, and it has only two allies: stress and depression, a powerful crew instrumental in helping grief conquer its quest. We must grab it by the tail to regain control! We simply can't give in without a good fight, at least a struggle.

"Come on, wipe your eyes and be strong for your man. You know he has a good heart."

Carol gathered herself, wiping the tears from her eyes as her mind continued to uncontrollably race, thinking, "How can we possibly beat the odds on this one? He's got all the cards!"

"Carol told her mom, 'I'll be okay; I really appreciate having you in my life.'" She went on to say, "Mike needs me! I'm going back home to console him."

Carol hugged and kissed her mom and walked out of the house; tears rolled down her cheeks as she got into the car.

Behind the door sat her mother with her back to the door, in prayer. "Lord, I have never asked you for anything; all I've ever done was praise your holy name and gave thanks for keeping your arms around me! I have always been your loyal servant. Lord, I need your safety net now! Provide them with your suit of armor so that no harm can penetrate. Turn them around, oh Lord! Show them the light that offers eternal life; in your name, Jesus Christ, I pray. Amen."

She didn't have the strength to rise from the floor at that moment, so she sat there for a while, sobbing in tears.

Carol drove home in good spirits! Someone came to her in a still voice and said, "It's going to be alright! I'll put instruments in your path that'll help guide you the way! Don't waver…"

That infinite voice was all it took to convince her they were going to walk through the eye of the storm and not get wet. Although a little turbulence would occur from time to time, it too would conveniently dissipate and blow over.

Chapter 23

Mike and Jerry were walking on eggshells. They had to be extremely careful with every critical step taken; it reminded them of transporting a grenade everywhere they went with the plug extracted, compelling them to maintain a certain amount of applied pressure to prevent an explosion. Quite obviously, with one hand occupied, that left only one to operate; the scales were definitely unbalanced, but they had to take what they could get! All's fair in love and war.

Carol parked the car in the driveway and made her way to the door. When she opened the door, Mike was sitting at the kitchen table, eating a bowl of dry cereal and watching the news on the flat-screen TV mounted on the wall. His spirit was incredibly inspirational!

He picked up his cell, dialing Carol's cell, and a ring indicated a text message.

Mike, with emphasis supplied, said, "I was thinking while you were away at your mom's house; he has to keep that 'joy stick,' as he calls it, close, considering we're under 24-hour watch. We have to be vigilant! We need to get someone inside to find out where he keeps it.

"We may have to plant our people in there and have them figure out where he keeps the remote control; damn! That's crazy! A remote control that operates our behinds! Another possible option we have is to seek out a private doctor who can help us remove the device! Of course, there are more options, but those are the ones that jump off the page now as we speak. I'm good! It's a quest, but we're going to be okay!"

The second she acknowledged the message, it was deleted—part of the plan to prevent senseless errors! The devil is a lie! "We won't make mistakes…"

"Carol: I love you, Boo!"

That Monday, before Mike and Jerry reported to Mr. Banks, they made sure Carol and Sherry had their itineraries secured. Contacting the banks, organizing the crews for rehab, servicing rental agreements, sending blast emails out to real estate consumers about the discount pricing on their properties; after that was done, they planned to go on the internet and find a specialist capable of removing the devices tucked inside them and Jerry.

Sherry and Carol couldn't wait to get started, anticipating the difficult journey ahead, trying to find a gutsy surgeon capable of removing a device of that nature; especially considering it was something usually handled by the United States Government!

"It's going to be extremely difficult moving on sheer instinct, choosing the right doctor," Carol said. "The Lord spoke to me! He said, 'My child! All you have to do is believe in me, and through me, all things are possible.'"

They'd contacted several doctors; they all told them to alert the Federal Government, and they would get the DEA on it immediately. They have a law—the Antiterrorism Death Penalty Act—especially for cases that involve organized crime, drug kingpins, and terrorism!

Sherry convinced the doctors not to disclose any information, knowing he had power invested in him to rival the government. Even worse, if the information recklessly seeped out, four people would lose their lives!

"Doctor Freeman: I have to be quite honest with you; the thought of opening the incision is frightening in itself. There's absolutely no way to determine if the device has a sensor that triggers an explosion if tampered with! So you see, dear, there are lots of variables that have to be considered in the process. I want to encourage you to contact the FBI. My question here is, don't you think it would be better to contact the best source available to help save your lives instead of using your own amateur wits to handle this problem alone?"

"Carol: Doc, I got to tell you this is a well-organized drug cartel responsible for this horrendous, ridiculous, diabolical act of extortion and will go to any length to achieve their goal! It's our guess he has strong ties to the FBI."

As soon as this information hit the desk, the button got pushed, and two people were instantly stopped by the hands of yours truly maniacs who had a total disregard and disrespect for the laws of our society. Banks had connections in every crack imaginable—not just in New York City, but the entire United States!

"It wouldn't surprise me if these guys haven't broken bread with Biden: they are esteemed representatives carrying signature titles of prestigious, influential entrepreneurs who have made a mark with their uniquely remarkable brand! They probably went to school with the guy. All I know is the man has a wealth of power!"

She went on to say, "It sounds like a really good idea to consult the proper authority, but the final decision is not hers to decide. I will talk with them to see if they're susceptible to good advice!"

The girls continued calling doctors, hoping to find someone who was empathetic and willing to stick his neck out for them!

Mike and Jerry were on their way to the Banks estate to see what was brewing.

"Jerry: Mike, you know we probably wouldn't be in this mess if you hadn't gone ballistic, getting controversial! You should have downplayed the incriminating information we had against him until much later."

"Mike: You know, Jerry, I was thinking the same thing, but you know something? Maybe it just wasn't meant to happen that way. Everything happens for a reason. The only thing we can do now, as we went over many times, is: 'The rabbit has the gun, but if we feed him enough carrots laced with mercy, he'll eventually fall over and die.' We got to stay focused! We don't have the luxury to fumble. When we come off that pivot, we have to go for the slam dunk shot that breaks the glass."

As they greeted security, pulling onto the premises, their Adam's apple dropped, wondering what he had planned for them.

The first knock on the door had him walking down the hall behind "us," allowing him space to open his door. He welcomed them in and courteously offered seats.

"Banks: Good evening! How was your weekend?"

"Mike: I got to be honest, it was crazy! Being monitored and strapped with a bomb 24/7 isn't something you can avoid thinking about—how it will affect the rest of our lives."

"Banks: Well! I'll tell you what. Here are cell phones; when either of these phones rings, you must answer immediately! Also, in about 10 minutes, Bruno and Jarvis are going to take you out to the shooting range to make sure you are thorough. Once you have satisfied your trainer, I have a martial arts instructor coming in to teach you how to adequately defend yourselves in hand-to-hand combat!"

Bruno and Jarvis walked into Mr. Banks' office, and he explained to them what weapons he wanted them to use in the training process, which included role play on how to install C4. Jerry looked at Mike and said, "They must be preparing us for some real serious drama. First they put bombs inside of us; now they're teaching us hand-to-hand combat and how to put C4s under cars, trucks, and buildings. Are we ready for this?"

"Do we have a choice?" Jerry replied. "I guess that answers your question."

Mike pulled over to read what Jerry texted: "I can't believe they have the audacity to teach us their strategies on how to defend ourselves against them; this is some gangster shit! I'm going to take advantage of this course for sure." Mike laughed as he turned on the music.

Jerry got a call on the cell Banks gave him earlier that day. He answered!

"Banks: I hope you boys are not entertaining any crazy notions. You're in tall grass; eyes are everywhere. The devices are well secured and under gate watch by someone not even close to this establishment, waiting for my command or the next person in charge if I'm unavailable, incapacitated, and can't work the controls! We'll see you guys tomorrow! Have a nice day!"

He hung up.

Chapter 24

"Jerry: That was Banks threatening to kill us if we try anything foolish. He said he has this guy who steps in if anything should happen to him. He becomes Chief Commander responsible for us. Plus, he said something about the device not being at their location! Someone else is monitoring us and making daily, up-to-the-minute reports!"

Mike was in awe because that reminded him how sensitively intense their situation was. When they finally arrived back home from a long day of training, they learned Sherry and Carol had spent the entire day working the lines and googling to get answers!

Carol flipped open her cell to text. She told Mike about the thoughts they had posing as two women seeking employment to get into his office and kill him, but that was a fleeting dumb moment knowing Banks delegated someone else to monitor them. "He's too busy to sit and play with a joystick. He has to tend to other aspects of the business!"

Sherry thought it would be ingenious to get into Pleasure Island Resort somehow to find out how often they were being watched. "Carol and I said we were going to discuss it with the two of you to see what you think." They bounced it around using the best tool available (text). Jerry said, "Let's sleep on it to allow time to explore the pros and cons!"

"Carol: Before we go home, I almost forgot to mention a private doctor told me that it could be very dangerous to attempt to go this alone; besides, there's not a doctor in the United States who would touch this without a bomb expert by his side to defuse it! I didn't want to tell you guys at the risk of you getting depressed again."

They all locked into one another's terrifying eyes and saw unity and an overwhelming determination to prevail! Carol and Sherry could see the clench in Mike and Jerry's jaws. They could see through the skin their teeth grinding with revenge.

Jerry held his cell up in the air and motioned to Sherry, "Let's go home." As soon as Jerry walked in the door, Mike called to remind him they had to call Dino and Do Good to drop off the package and pick up 24k at Johnnie's spot. When they got there, Jerry told the brothers, "We have access to a great deal more, and we can supply you with whatever you can hold down! How much can you move in a week?"

"Do Good," clearing his throat in the midst of the excitement, hurried to speak through the throat irritation, "We can handle as much as you can drop on the table; son! We're the real 'BALLERS!' We handle our business well outside the paint without pass interference; you happen to be rolling with the best, baby! Kobe can take a back seat on this one."

"Mike: After you work those two keys, we're coming back with a double up so you can really make your chatter. You ready, playboy?"

"Dino: Man! Come on with that movement. Don't be late! For sure!"

Mike and Jerry returned to their last day of boot camp to find two 30-shot 9 mm with extra clips and silencers to muffle the dangerously violent annoyance and unwanted attention every time a round was fired. Turning to look at one another while Banks continued to give instructions, he told them there were going to be two guys in hotel room 645 at the Holiday Inn Elect at the airport location.

"Are you familiar?" They responded together, "Yes, sir!" looking astute and assiduous as though they'd been vintage hitmen for quite some time.

"Banks: I know no explanations are necessary, but the two guys I want you to hit are 'painters,' snitchers, and word has come down from Washington, D.C., to all crime bosses to get them at all costs; otherwise, some strong players will take a fall. They're not the least bit suspicious. We know they've rolled over, so approach the room as waiters employed by the hotel, sent to shower them with special perks of the hotel—the best wine in the venue! We furnished them with a plush two-bedroom with all hotel accommodations and two beautiful hookers, not to be harmed in any way; they are two of our finest ladies from Florida."

Mike and Jerry, like twins grasping at the same thought, thought, "He has the audacity to make us atrocious, compelling us to perpetrate masked murder and become notorious drug lords."

"Could it be because we're black residents of the city? No, that wasn't an option!"

"Banks asked: Do either of you have any questions?"

"Jerry: As a matter of fact, I do have a question. What gives you the foggiest impression we are murderers? What prompts you to think we'll follow through with these crazy, notorious murder and extortion plots? What crystal ball are you looking in that says we'll be successful?"

"Banks: It's your life or theirs! The choice is yours!"

"Jerry: Mannnnnn," with a long pause, "when you have a bundle of dynamite stuck in your underwear, you don't have a choice. Consider it done! Where do we dispose of the burners?"

"Banks: Throw them in the river. Now! On Tuesday at 9:45 PM sharp, I want you knocking on 645. The girls should have the informants higher than a kite and screwing their brains out; it's your job to maneuver your way into the room! Is that all?"

"Yes!"

"I'll give you a call soon. You can excuse yourselves. Oh! When the job is done, call and let it ring until the answering machine picks up and says 'mission accomplished,' then hang up."

His bodyguards posted up in his office with ugly mugs; this was really tugging at everybody's heartstrings—suspenseful, not knowing what to do!

They had exactly 24 hours to conjure a really good idea of how to execute their plan. Sharing this mind-blowing plot with anyone outside of him and Jerry would knock the breath out of them to think they'd become monstrous hitmen for a mob and couldn't turn back the hands on the clock.

The bottom line was they absolutely didn't want Carol and Sherry to ever fully acknowledge the magnitude of the bottomless pit they'd fallen ten tiers down and counting! Especially considering they had no clue what kind of roller coaster ride they were strapped on, with strict denial to access an emergency release.

Chapter 25

The next day at precisely 9:30—fifteen minutes earlier to get in the lobby and get positioned! Discretely navigating their way through to prevent any engagement or encounter, they noticed a phone in a hallway. Mike picked it up and dialed 654. A lady answered the phone.

"Mike: This is the front desk! I'm calling on behalf of The Holiday Inn Elect to make sure you found your room okay and that you are satisfied with the rooms. I would also like to inform you that according to your rental agreement, you are entitled to all hotel accommodations free. Is there anything we can get for you—food, soft drinks, or maybe an alcoholic beverage of your choosing to romantically proceed with your evening?"

She implied yes! Asking everyone what they wanted to order via hotel free accommodations! Considering they'd just taken the girls out to a good steakhouse restaurant, "Momma's Steak to Go," they ordered that new "Diva Absolute" and orange juice.

"Mike: Be right up!"

Jerry very gracefully went to the bar and purchased a fifth of Hennessy and a bottle of orange juice!

Mike held the elevator with seconds before 9:45! Jerry got on the elevator to the 6th floor. The door opened, looking for room 645.

"Jerry: This way!"

Mike grabbed a tray he saw sitting on the sideline, got a bucket of ice, and two hotel jackets that conveniently hung on a rack. The waiter politely knocked on the door. Seconds later, one of the men answered.

"We didn't order room service!"

One of the girls interrupted, "Yes, we did! You were in the bedroom with Jessica, preoccupied."

He said, "Please come in!"

Mike humbly pushed the tray in, and Jerry grabbed the guy's attention, saying something funny. He started advancing towards Jerry. The second he was in reaching distance, he opened his hand, hitting him in his throat, disabling him. Quickly, with the other hand, he poked him in both eyes, causing blood to run profusely.

"He yells, 'Something's wrong!'" At that point, Mike shot him in the chest. The bedroom door swung open. Before he could aim, Jerry shot him in the mouth and multiple times in the heart. He fell to the bed, choking on his blood, dying almost instantly!

The two girls had no involvement with registration. Mike and Jerry sort of stared at the two girls with a dare-you look. Quickly, they exited the hotel room, fading into the shadows as though it never happened! They wore gloves, but you can't be sure unless you're sure, so they wiped off everything they'd touched while in the room.

Exiting the room, they hopped on the closest elevator to ground level, heading out a side door. They went panting from the adrenaline rush, pumped up to commit an unthinkable, unexplainable, and unjustifiable homicide that couldn't be reversed! Sewing themselves back together from the devastation, they knew the next stop was the river to dump the burners.

"Mike: Dang, Jerry! You act like you like this shit! You could have handled them both by yourself."

"Jerry: It's kill or be killed; no in between. Those guys probably underwent the same professional lethal training. You better get with the program!"

"Mike: Pausing! You're right!"

The next day at 12:00 PM, check-out time, the cleanup personnel opened the door, assuming they'd checked out, to find two dead bodies! The Mexican housekeeping lady hysterically rushed to tell her manager. She didn't think to call the front desk; she hurried out of the room!

The manager went into the room and backed out because he didn't want to interfere with the police department's investigation! No one in the hotel knew or suspected anything out of the ordinary.

The room was paid for with a Visa stolen from a person earlier at a department store!

On the six o'clock news, it was reported two men were killed at the Airport Holiday Inn Elect Hotel, coming into the New Year, January 1, 2011, at 12:00 PM. The two men were just now identified as Carl Donavan and Steven Edison, co-owners of "Crowns Jeweler"!

So far, there are no suspects, but be assured there will be a thorough ongoing investigation to resolve this senseless, cold-blooded murder that appears to be for hire! Unfortunately, we can't give any more information at this time because the investigation may be compromised.

Before the newscast, Mike dropped Jerry off at home, then headed straight home. Walking through the door, Carol and Sherry were watching a televised production of the crime scene at the Holiday Inn on the news!

Mike and Jerry sat down on the couch, very attentive to pinpoint any unscrupulous mistakes they could have made as first-time amateurs, shocked to find they were extorted and compelled to kill two men.

Every criminal act they were forced to execute was being recorded in a diary to someday reflect on and share with others to prevent against things of this insane nature.

Meanwhile, while they were watching the news broadcast, pondering a way out, Dino and Do Good were at the crap house rolling the dice with intentions of recruiting. Reflecting on the conversation with Mike and Jerry about a larger shipment coming in, they figured the more recruits, the better!

Strength was in numbers. After leaving the crap house, they surveyed the neighborhood in the mean streets of Harlem to find potential spots to set up shop for the massive movement.

At the end of the day, three apartments were rented and nine brothers inducted into the family!

The plan was to put three to a unit with a surveillance system that monitored movement around the entire unit. The units were upstairs and downstairs with fake plug outlets installed in each unit that went from one unit into the other; a method used to give the false impression that the drugs were being secreted in the downstairs unit when instead, it was upstairs.

The customers would never learn we get it through a hole in the wall! That way, if they ran into a customer who was unfortunately caught by the law and rolled over, becoming a painter, they didn't want him to be able to give accurate details, knowing to acquire a search warrant includes specific detailed information on where the drugs could be found in the home!

Plus, the operation would move to another location every ninety days to prevent complacency and effective investigations from taking place by the DEA or other special task forces.

Dino and his brother were stepping back a few feet to let their team handle the street productivity! A job isn't complete without all its proper ingredients.

The zero-tolerance boys needed some heat to keep the riffraff down! No one was going to make a come-up off these boys! Roughnecks to the core!

Mike dialed the number to inform that the mission was complete and hung up. He got a call back as soon as he hung up.

"Mr. Banks: I called you back to extend my appreciation for a job well done; the girls told us you guys did excellent. I'm really amazed at how well you conducted yourselves. The training really paid off handsomely."

"Mike: Considering we served you well, what is the possibility of you having these devices removed at some point?"

"Banks: We'll have to see about that. It depends! If you keep up the good work, it can only enhance the chances of a reconsideration, or should I say reprieve. Oh! By the way, this coming Saturday, I have another job arranged for the two of you; we have a concert scheduled the same day, but I would first like to meet with the two of you to discuss the plan; then you can go hang out and enjoy our first concert here, featuring Keri Hilson, Trey Songs, Usher, Snoop Dogg, Dirty Money, Jamie Foxx as MC, Carrie Underwood, and Selena Gomez, a new favorite breakout artist who'll blow you away! Jamie Foxx wowed the audience with his new comedic material—the mistaken blind pushers in prison, the jokes about the blind man who worked out daily in the prison gym, and the triple awesome blind boxers with no below-the-belt penalties! He embellished his presentation with hilarious talks about 'no pity in the court system'—how they will lock up the blind, crippled, and crazy, and even people who unfortunately don't have legs or arms with severe hearing disabilities!

"Seats are $100.00 with two concerts Saturday and Sunday because we sold twice our capacity! Banks went on to say he thought it was largely due to the different styles of music presented. I can go on, but let's get down to business first. I have five keys here. What I want you to do is put this on the street. Your cut of the take is 30%, and mine is 70%. I definitely don't have a problem with your application, as I'm sure you have savvy in this line of work; numbers don't lie."

They were excited to learn it wasn't another murder plot.

"Mike: I'm glad you're at least giving us an opportunity to earn a living! We have eleven guys on the streets of Harlem 24/7 pounding the pavement, working our product with due diligence. They all have zero-tolerance attitudes and are well-respected by their peers and all the OGs!"

"Banks: It sounds like you have a good operation with a strong backbone. Here's your package and two tickets, compliments of Pleasure Island Resort to the concert; enjoy yourselves!"

They put the keys in two briefcases and took them to Grandma's place until the concert was over. While at the concert, it gave them an opportunity to talk without scrutiny!

They didn't have to text with the noise pollution! Banks provided them with VIP seats; I guess this is his strange way of showing his appreciation for us taking care of his dirty laundry that warrants a life sentence in prison or the death penalty. I can't say we're lucky because either way, we're doomed! Damned if you do and damned if you don't. It certainly stirs curiosity about what's in that stew. One thing is for sure: the ingredient was incredibly explosive!

"Mike: To make the product work, we have to first step on it at least twice, rock it up, and give it to Dino and Do Good to sell eight balls, halves, and 'O's; otherwise, the money won't quite pan out considering the margins put in place by Banks!"

"Jerry: Man, our lives sure have taken a detour down a path of uncertainty. We don't know if this ride will ever end or what shape we'll be in at the finish line; this is a really tragic situation! I think all we have to do is convince him that we like this shit, and he'll probably change his whole perspective. Then, once he's rocked to sleep, we can find that device; we've got to play our 'A Game!'"

"Mike: You make a lot of sense! That may be our only venue considering 'you keep your enemy closer!' Yeah! Let's charm this snake! Jerry: This concert is off the chain! Banks and his boys' marketing strategies are off the Richter scale, intertwining new artists Selena Gomez and Carrie Underwood in with the current rap and R&B artists capable of drawing consumers from everywhere! Plus, it affords the opportunity to get an audience on both sides of the aisle, which definitely means more ticket sales? Man, check Jamie Foxx out; he's crazy. I think we better get out of here to beat the crowd."

Chapter 26

While this was going on, Banks and Wiggins were in the office talking about their Colombian connection! How the Colombians are moving cocaine in submarines right now, as we speak, to the Qudamola Shores, then using zip lines and backpacks to transport it through the jungle for pennies on the dollar; at the risk of being bitten by a snake or slaughtered by a wild animal in its natural habitat!

Early that next morning (Sunday), Mike called Jerry. "Man, let that bed go! We've got to get cracking. We have to get to the store and buy baking soda to rock that stuff."

"Jerry: Yeah! You're right! Give me about an hour. That'll give me enough time to work my hygiene magic and grab a bite to eat."

When Jerry arrived in front of the house, he called Mike's cell phone.

"Mike: Yeah!"

"Jerry: I'm outside!"

"Mike: I'm walking out now!"

They went straight to the store and purchased 20 boxes of baking soda from 10 different stores with the sole intent to minimize any possible suspicion! After this was done, their next steps were to rock four birds and keep one powder specifically for cocaine customers who didn't smoke crack.

Jerry flipped his cell open and dialed Do Good's number. Do Good's answering machine picked up.

"What they do, what they do, hit me back!"

Jerry called again, and Do Good picked up.

"Do Good: Word! What's up!"

"Jerry: I got that good!"

"Do Good: Man, we were impatiently waiting on you guys to get back in the scheme of things! You know we're holding down nine young brothers ready to mix and mingle with anything that comes their way; they're down-home boys!"

"Jerry: That's the play! Strength is in numbers, and numbers don't lie. The meeting place was the Henson brothers' home this time!"

When they arrived, Dino told them that they had three apartments upstairs and down ready to go; all they needed was the product!

Mike pulled the package out of the briefcase and began discussing numbers. Reaching an agreement, Jerry gave the brothers two birds. As Jerry extended his hand to give him the package, he asked, "How long do you think it'll take your team to knock this off?"

"Do Good: About ten days, give or take a day or two! We'll shake down every spot in this town if we have to, but you know we won't have a problem because we got that good!"

Dino made connections with their boys before the meeting concluded when the phone rang. Rob picked up.

"Dino: Hello! Can I speak with Rob?"

"This is Rob! What's up, dirty?" He recognized Dino looking at his caller ID.

"Dino: I got something for you!"

"Rob: That sounds like a winner! Come on with that!"

"Dino: We're still working at a seventy-thirty cut. We'll meet with you guys in two hours at your apartment."

He hung up and called "Blunt and Throw Down" with the same proposition; they both agreed! They were ready to roll. Dino and his brother went to purchase nine thirty-shot 9mm and three AKs from a gun racket famous for stealing guns from trains and breaking into gun stores to snatch the most powerful weapons on display. Who cared where they came from? They were disposable once used!

Later that day, Banks called Mike at home to check if everything was working out okay.

"Mike: Yeah! It's working out just fine. In fact, we have a large crew with three apartment buildings to put our work in!"

"Banks: Good! I'm so glad to hear that! Listen, I want you and Jerry to come in tomorrow! I have another business arrangement for the two of you."

"Mike: Is there any special time you want us there?"

"Banks: Yes! Let's try for 8:00 PM."

"Mike: We'll be there! I hope you are noticing we're on our best behavior. This thing inside of us keeps us on edge."

Banks offered no comment.

When they arrived the next day, they were told they would be taking a trip to Orlando, Florida.

"Once you arrive, you are to catch a cab to 4156 Spencer Dr. You will meet with a lady named Samantha Willis. She will inform you what to do from there. Your flight is scheduled to leave at 3 PM on Tuesday, and your return flight is set for Wednesday at 5 PM."

On Tuesday, they boarded the plane, pursuing their next quest.

Discretely innovative in their approach to find out who was following them on this trip, Mike and Jerry cautiously gauged to see if anyone was familiar as they were humbly escorted to their seats. A gut feeling told them they were under surveillance from the sky!

They knew big brother had a front-row seat! They could feel his eerie presence! They intuitively knew staying under the radar was not an option.

"We strapped in," and Jerry pulled his phone from his hip.

"Jerry: The only thing we can do is ride this mystery out! One thing's for sure; when we get to the other end, the mystery will be dispelled right before our eyes! We can feel the turbulence; the plane just hit the runway."

"Mike: You're right! It won't be long now. When we meet this Samantha person, she might hand us another bomb; that'll be crazy picking up a bomb when we already have one!"

"Jerry: Man, you got jokes!"

As they walked through the terminal to get their luggage, they noticed the baggage disposal terminating luggage out of a chute that spun around.

"Jerry: Here it is right here!"

Grabbing their luggage, they exited the airport to catch a cab to the address given by Banks. After twenty minutes, they pulled into a driveway with a security booth and a gorgeous, huge security gate that slowly opened at the gatekeeper's command. The estate was a beautiful white home trimmed in pink. The landscaping was phenomenal—like nothing they'd ever seen! It was absolutely surreal!

They walked up to a tall door tailor-made for Magic Johnson and rang the bell. The unusually loud ding-dongs bounced off the walls.

Samantha had a horse stable almost identical to the one at Mr. Banks' estate. A beautiful lady appeared at the door and asked, "Please come in! My name is Sabrina! How may I help you, handsome young men?"

A delayed response came over them! They were in awe, mesmerized by her overwhelming, incapacitating beauty. She was a firecracker!

Chapter 27

"Sabrina: I think she's expecting you! You guys can have a seat! She'll be right down!"

Turning to walk away, they couldn't help but notice her strong, sexy legs that were well-defined. Mike and Jerry thought introspectively, "I wonder what she looks like when she's wearing nothing?"

Samantha suddenly appeared, walking down a long flight of stairs, greeting them.

"Hi, gentlemen! I was expecting you. You must be Michael and Jerry?"

"That's correct!"

"Samantha: Please! Come with me so I can give you the details."

Walking out of the foyer through a hallway revealing huge open rooms; in one room, they noticed a familiar face. They recognized Mr. Wiggins, co-owner of Boatmen's Bank, the same guy who extended them the loan; thinking quietly, "He must be connected with the operation too."

Finally entering the office, Samantha sat behind her cherry oak desk with matching chairs and asked them to "please have a seat."

"Samantha: I have a thorn in my side, and I need your help to remove it. I run a multimillion-dollar industry, and nothing stands in my way to success! I have a young lady who has worked for me for three years, and she's very special. Unfortunately, she has met an annoying young punk who has become a distraction to the business. He's trying to get her out of the business and encourages her to shortchange the company's till! That's totally prohibited. I want him dead!

If the other girls find out it's that easy to break free, I'll lose credibility, and my entire franchise will crumble right before my eyes; I may as well get out of the game. I want him dead!

I want you to go to the airport with my maid and rent a car using your credit card! You will be reimbursed! I want you to take this C4 that you were trained to use and attach it underneath the car. Carefully secure it on the driver side. This device here is the transmitter! When he gets in the car and it's in motion, push and "call it a wrap."

Michelle, my maid, will take you to the airport. The bomb and transmitter will be packaged and stored in the trunk of her car. Before taking you to the airport, she'll take you by Edgar's Sports Bar, where he goes to almost every night. He'll definitely be there. Oh! Be sure to request a GPS so you won't get lost. We don't make mistakes!

My friends and I are flying out to Chicago today. Our flight is scheduled to leave at 4:30 PM. It has really been a pleasure meeting you, although we may never meet again. I want to thank you in advance for a thorough job performance. Robert told me that you were really good and very dependable; I'm sure he'll pay you a very handsome number!

Again, I want to thank you! I have to be leaving expeditiously."

What she conveniently failed to tell them was that the organization hired Thomas to move product, and he failed to do so, falling prey to the masterful king and queen of destruction, "cocaine and heroin," whose new boss he is; and even more insulting, he's been spotted talking to the DEA on numerous occasions! That's the genuine reason for his execution!

They all left the premises together, with Mike and Jerry riding with Michelle to the sports bar. She told them exactly what kind of car he'd be driving, along with a license plate number, so there'd be no mistake.

She even gave a detailed description of Thomas, the boyfriend. Afterwards, she took them to the airport to get transportation from Avis Rent a Car. Later that night, contemplating the thought of another murder, they realized, "We have become mass murderers!"

One mind kept telling them not to go through with it, and the other side of the cerebellum told them to go ahead! Banks wins again!

The man who has absolutely no idea hasn't done anything wrong that deserves a death sentence without a chance to defend himself against the allegations pending. Stopping at a service station to borrow a pen, Mike wrote down two names: "Samantha Willis and Ralph Wiggins," showing it to Jerry. Then he texted, "These are two important names we need to record for future reference!"

At 8:30 that night, they were sitting in the car about 50 feet from the sports bar. Jerry rolled under the car, attached the bomb underneath, and waited. An hour and a half later, Thomas walked out of the pub with three friends—two guys and a girl—who all walked incoherently to the car, waiting for Thomas to unlock the doors.

He hit the remote, unlocking the car, and they all piled in!

Mike, holding the transmitter in his hand, was not sure what to do, indecisively torn between right and wrong; the car began to accelerate with Mike still frozen, not knowing what to do! Jerry quickly snatched it away and immediately pressed the button to activate; the car instantly blew, taking a leap through the air.

They pulled off as the car continued to burn with helpless people inside, horribly suffering as they incinerated in flames.

"Mike: Utters 'another heinous murder in the first degree! This'll be branded in my mind for the duration of my life, coupled with the ugly collection of unthinkable murders secretly hidden in the archives of my mind!'"

The news interrupted with an important news flash: "Four people were killed minutes ago in a car bombing at Jason's Sports Bar at 1123 Delmar. The police chief is adamant this murder was a hit for hire based on the caliber of explosives and technique used on the AKA Shop Stewart, a notorious drug dealer famous for his recidivism in committing unconscionable drug deals! Transparency should have been the first name given. He makes his transactions like a child going into a candy store to purchase candy right in the presence of everyone, like what he's doing is morally right!

Center stage for the world's eyesore entertainment; boy has he screwed up this time!

Chapter 28

Mike and Jerry were given strict orders to kill him and destroy the transmitter after the job was finished; they did exactly that! At 5 PM, they turned in the rental and caught a shuttle to the airport; at 5 PM sharp, they were boarding a plane back to New York, Manhattan!

Getting on the plane, still shaken from the murders, they looked around inconspicuously to spot a familiar face, but unfortunately to no avail! Though they both had a dose of paranoia playing its antics before landing because a lady and a man reminded them of someone perhaps they'd seen on their way back from Florida.

"Jerry: I think we're too paranoid. Let's change the subject! What do you think Sherry and Carol are doing? I can't wait to get home."

"Mike: I can't either!" looking out the window.

While Mike and Jerry were in flight, Dino was at the shopping mall flossing, getting his NY swag on. He met an old buddy he knew when he was in prison named Darby Bey, a Moorish American; he had been released from prison only a week. They welcomed one another with a warm embrace and a big smile of excitement.

"Dino: You say you're out a week!"

"Darby: Yeah, man!"

"Dino: It must feel good just to walk down the street, knock on someone's door, walk into a mall, or pump your own gas. Not to mention getting that hot, steamy opportunity to explode inside some fine woman!"

"Darby: She doesn't have to be good-looking either! I just want to release! Hey! I got a job at McDonald's; what are you doing, Dino? You're looking good, playa; life's been kind to you!"

"Dino: I have been working for some friends rehabbing properties. These brothers are innovators, overzealously motivated! Plus, you know I got to get my street on. We can all use some supplemental income. Let me give you my digits!"

"Darby: I don't have a cell, but you can pick me up at mom's house. The number is 362-8866!"

"Dino: What do you say I stop in later tonight and take you to Club Flamingo? It's on me! Those fools will have you rolling, plus there are a lot of cute honeys!"

"Darby: That sounds like it'll be 'Animalistic!' I'm all in! Where's your brother, Do Good?"

"He's probably at home or making an urgent run. He'll be with me tonight! We got some young, loyal, determined brothers you got to meet; after your vacation, maybe we can hook up and get you back in the mix. It's your call! Just give me a yell when you're ready. I'll see you later! I have to catch some of these calls to get my paper chase on."

Dino gets in the car and pulls off, headed to one of his dope houses. As he parallel parks, talking on the phone to "Throw Down," he was multitasking, selling a 50-cent piece. Dino parked, watching the transaction unfold. Throw Down was passing off the 50, and the "clucker" magically made the switch almost as fast as Throw Down could pass it to him, like the famous three-card molly played by the best in the business!

He pretended to look at it and handed it back to Throw Down, saying, "This is too small; can you do better than this?"

Dino smiled because he knew his boy caught the switch. He let it play out! Throw Down accepted the package, analyzing to realize it definitely wasn't the package he had given him. He told the guy, "No problem!" At that same instance, he snatched him into the apartment and took him upstairs by gunpoint. He opened the package on a table in the hallway, revealing wax.

He looked the guy in the eye and said, "That's okay!" Backhanding him with his 9mm, knocking him down a flight of stairs! As he rolled past Dino, he kicked him several times, propelling his fall. While he rolled from top to bottom, Throw Down was cursing, "The next time you come with that lame horse manure, they're going to find your happy ass in a trash can with that same hand you made the switch with cut off and stuck in your ass!"

"Dino: What's happening here?"

"Throw Down: This lame tried to pull a switch on me. I got to have my paper."

After he explained what had happened, Dino told him, "Have your boys take over the shop later around 6 PM so you can get your curb appeal straight; we're going to Club Flamingo. I have someone I want you to meet."

"He's a big asset!"

Throw Down called Rob and Blunt on his cell while they were out making runs collecting money.

"Rob answers! Yeah! What's up!"

"Throw Down: I want to bring you guys up to speed. There have been changes in the plan; Dino wants me to roll with him later. He didn't say why, and I didn't particularly care!"

"Rob: Cool, man! We got this. You guys be careful out there!"

"Throw Down: Word! Meet us at the club about 9 PM. As a matter of fact, why don't you guys shut down at about 8 PM and meet us at Club Flamingo. The club!"

"We'll be there…"

Chapter 29

Throw Down told Dino that he let his boys off early to meet us at the club; they could use a little "me time!" At 8:30, they went to pick up Darby Bey. For the first time in nine years, he was walking into a club; all the honeys were checking him out like he was a fresh, tasty steak smothered with delicious gravy, anxious to be served.

Dino and Do Good were eye candy as well. All of the cuties were crazy about their swagger, plus they had awesome respect. A few minutes later, walking through the door, waiting to be patted down by security, noticing Dino, Do Good, and Throw Down sitting at a booth with room reserved! That's what I call "good-looking!"

Gracefully, they worked their way through the crowded club, unable to successfully avoid bumping into people, finally making it to their party. Little Rob and Blunt worked their way through the crowd to get closer to the stage to hear the comedians; Dino, Do Good, and brother Darby Bey continued sitting at the booth dialoguing and listening to the comedians' funny jokes!

Darby Bey couldn't go anywhere because he'd gotten an erection sitting there, watching those fine young women dressed so eloquently in their nicely shaped, fitted ensembles! Wearing mascara that made their eyes say, "Take me to bed with you tonight!" It was so unfortunate he wore boxers instead of briefs. He couldn't hold it down; it was embarrassing!

He was so horny! With the slightest shift of the wind, he'd get aroused! Sitting there in a temporary, relapsed, institutionalized state of mind, thinking it's a violation to stare at a woman too long because in prison they write you up for "reckless eyeballing" for staring at a female guard.

Darby Bey snapped out of his trance and told Dino the inside jokes. They both laughed!

"Dino: Man, prison sure can make a person institutionalized. After you live that lifestyle for so long, you'll get past that in just a few sessions with these honeys; trust me!"

A lady approached him and said, "I couldn't help noticing you sitting here; let me guess, you're married!"

"Darby Bey: No! Why do you say that?"

"Christina: Because you've been sitting here for quite some time and haven't said anything to any of the women in the club."

He implied, "That's primarily because I haven't seen anyone that put that twinkle in my eye until you appeared from nowhere! It's a blessing! My name is Julius Darby! My Moorish brothers call me Darby Bey; what's your name, sweetheart?"

"Christina Jazz!"

"Julius: Do you come here often?"

"Christina: Maybe twice a month on comedy nights."

"Julius: Are you married or single?"

She replies, "Single!" At that point, she opened the storybook to her life.

She explained how her boyfriend wanted her to always stay home, cook meals, and do all the other homely things; she didn't have a problem with that, but he didn't take care of her.

He seldom wanted to make love.

"We have sexual appetites stronger than men! Keri Hilson says, 'Every love has a limit.'"

He interrupted, "That's an understatement!"

She asks, "What do you mean?"

He responds, "I'll explain later; I don't want to distract your most moving yet intriguing thought."

She continues, "He treated me like I was nonexistent, so I started hanging out in the clubs until ungodly hours in the morning! I knew he would eventually assume I was fooling around on him, so he packed his bags, left, and never came back. Now back to your statement: 'It's an understatement,' what did you mean by that?"

"Julius: Earlier you mentioned women get just as hot as men. That jolted an instant thought that played around in my head. Nine years without sex is ridiculous! She must not know what that does to a man."

"Christina: Share it with me!"

"Julius: Well! To be quite honest, I was just released from prison, and I don't think there's a woman more sexually charged than I am right now. The reason I've glued myself to this seat is that I easily get hot and bothered by the slightest cast of the wind, after being held in prison for so long. Now, stumbling upon a charmingly beautiful woman engaging in conversation! The mere thought of that fantasy coming true prevents me from moving my hand from my crotch area; this is embarrassing! I am definitely ill-prepared for this outing."

As he continued to talk discreetly without permission, she irresistibly ran her hand underneath the table to sample his package!

"Oh boy! You're packing like a horse, big time!"

He forgot to mention it was "hard and big," bent in a big arch shape. The brother hung like a horse. Christina was a sharp shooter! She shot from the hip as you just witnessed. That was one notch she had to get under her belt. She wanted to smash Julius, just released from prison after serving nine years; "I apologize!" said Julius.

"Christina: No! No apology necessary; to be quite honest, I'm taken aback by this whole situation! You're incredibly interesting and an extremely attractive man. Very straightforward, she asked Julius, 'Let me be your dream girl. You deserve a good woman!'

"Let me take you to my home to avoid the hotel expenses and shower you with the love and affection you so righteously deserve. I'll take you to a place that'll make your eyes roll back in your head and your toes curl like super curly fries."

He anxiously looked around to find Dino or Do Good to let them know he was leaving with a friend. Signaling Dino, once he made it over to them, Julius introduced Dino to his new friend and mentioned that they were leaving together and he would call the next day.

Chapter 30

Once they arrived home in her Lexus, the garage door opened, and she slowly drove in with the door shutting behind them, heading straight to her plush bedroom with a huge flat-screen plasma TV.

Christina stood at 5'4", weighing 120 pounds, with hazel eyes. Her light skin complexion was complemented by brownish hair and a curvy, unimaginable body; she was fine! As they entered the bedroom, their clothes fell to the floor like profusely dripping sweat. She went into the kitchen and made herself a drink of tangerine and orange juice, setting one on the table for him.

She then hopped in the shower to refresh herself, having danced and gotten sweaty. She wanted to taste really good for Julius. The bathroom door opened, and she walked out wearing only a towel that covered the most interesting parts, leaving little to the imagination! He just knew this was a hit-and-run demo to let him hit it on the first day.

"Dang! The brother got swag, or Christina's hormones are running all over the place; either way, it didn't matter!"

She sat in the center of the bed, relaxed, partially propped up with her feet on the bed, her knees pointed to the ceiling, and her legs spread like the fork in the road, exposing one good-looking peach!

As he slowly crawled into the bed, setting her glass on the end table, he began to caress her wildly and very passionately! She was so absorbed in the moment that her eyes closed in submission as he proceeded to take Christina to another place, touching her with his wet tongue around the circumference of her tender spot!

He must have agitated something because that delicious, juicy peach was uncontrollably squirting all over the place for at least an hour; once she was seductively sedated, she was all his. He went inside the chambers of her walls like a true surgeon, very carefully and decisively, experiencing the joy and pleasure that he had sacrificed when he put himself in a precarious place that obviously landed him in prison; what a sacrifice!

This went on well into the next day; they were both totally exhausted from the extended hours of pure excitement, exercising vigorously like two exhibitionists trying to find that implosive pot of gold at the end of the rainbow! The next day, when he made it home, he called to tell Dino thanks for taking him out and treating him like a real blood brother.

"Dino picks up: Hello!"

"Julius: This is Darby Bey!"

"Dino: Hey! What's going on?"

"Julius: I just wanted to call and express my gratitude for showing a bro a nice time at the club. Plus! That honey I caught last night was hot as a muffler! She really has it going on… I hope it wasn't a drive-by; you know how these women are. They've gotten worse than us misguided fools, 'cause you know we're garden tools just waiting to pull a big juicy peach off a tree!"

The previous night at 10 PM, while they were at the club, Mike and Jerry were touching down on the runway; luckily, they moved through the airport to get their luggage with no problem! There weren't many people flying that day. They casually walked out of the airport talking and noticed a cab conveniently waiting, so they hopped in and gave the driver their destination request.

Jerry was dropped off first since he was nearer to the airport. They were exhausted from the improvised situation thrust upon them from the time they left until they returned home; every encounter or adventure was scary, not knowing what awaited at the end of the dark tunnel every time out.

When they made it home, Carol and Sherry were impatiently waiting for updates on their suspenseful journey plotted by Banks.

"Carol: How was the trip?"

"It was okay under the circumstances; he had Jerry and me dropping packages off at some pretty big businesses. One of them was a telemarketing company that offers a professional call girl ring behind the scenes. Baby, enough of that! What have you been doing?"

Banks just had to get an earful, because it was getting ready to get freaky in there.

Jerry and Sherry were a class act. They never made it off the couch! The next day, they crossed their fingers hoping Banks wouldn't call back after they reported the job was completed. They weren't energized to go back out on another mission. They were doing too much, knowing their luck would run out at some point.

They still went to work like two respectable businessmen. The supervisors were really crucial now because obviously, they didn't have time to supervise the supervisors! Banks kept them on the Amtrak.

The HUD homes were about complete. It was time for them to get back in the field to locate more properties and at least get some prospects!

Mike opened his cell to text with more information about this guy that might help them counteract his plan and dubiously escape his clutches. Right now, they had generated an overwhelming amount of incriminating evidence that would prevent anyone from harming a strain of hair on their heads; they had done literally everything asked, from moving drugs to murder.

Chapter 31

Months had passed, and he hadn't considered they had paid enough to have these devices removed. They were moving 15 birds a month, juggling like acrobats, moving from one apartment to another to keep the dog tracking scent down, so the police wouldn't be able to set up surveillance apparatuses.

Dino and Do Good had been turning corners right and left on a stroke of luck; as soon as the DEA set up shop, they vanished into thin air.

They had distribution centers north, east, south, and west. People would wait in line to be served powder or rock. The prostitutes were catching tricks simultaneously, trying to get back to see Scottie; some were so anxious they would run off with the "Johns' money because they were too impatient to complete the act! It wasn't about the trick; it was about the drug!

Young brothers were strung out, going in stores, taking merchandise, running or fighting their way out! It was called "rayfilling" when you snatched and ran. They were selling fake rings and chains that turned your neck and finger green if you wore them for a period of time. It was a crazy epidemic that spoke to millions of people from coast to coast; it had law-abiding citizens reluctant to leave their homes, and the red light machete bandit didn't make it any easier.

You could see the excitement when they were fortunate enough to make it through a yellow light without having to stop! They went from being excited about making it to work safe with all their limbs still attached!

Dino and Do Good seemed to have awakened every crack cocaine addict in New York City. They didn't carry guns like most drug dealers because not only had they earned a reputation in the game, but they also had a strong entourage that would crush the fire-breathing Goliath!

Sporting their twin BMWs, they fronted as though they didn't have a care in the world.

The following Saturday, Mike decided they would visit Grandma as planned, despite their differences with Mr. Banks; Carol and Sherry didn't like Banks. He was the most disgusting and exasperating! Still, they had to conduct themselves accordingly, pretending nothing happened.

His day would come when he put his "last quarter in the parking meter"! He certainly wouldn't dance on the dance floor.

Finally making it onto the premises,

"Jerry: I can smell something stewing already!"

They continued to drive through the maze to Grandma's house. Getting out of the car, laughing and kidding around, Jerry rang the bell. The door opened, and Grandma smiled like she hit the lottery; her smile was amazing!

In unison, they all said, "How are you doing, Grandma?" Before she could respond, hugs came from everywhere. One at a time, they embraced her with a special love so indescribable.

"Sherry implied: Have you been keeping up with the stock market?"

"Grandma: Now you know that's all I know! For the past twenty years, I've monitored the numbers as though it were my child. I know when to get in and when to pull back."

Mike intervened, telling her, "We really want to get to the stable before the sun goes down."

"Grandma: That's all you had to say! You kids get out of here. Enjoy yourselves, but be careful with those horses. I heard a little boy fell and broke his neck. The bridle wasn't tight enough or something!"

Chapter 32

Meanwhile, at the dope house, Blunt hired a young girl, 27 years old, to work the books for them because business was moving incredibly fast, and the astronomical numbers hitting the table were unthinkable. His primary concern was to ensure the numbers were correct, so a new twist came into the picture.

Janice was hired to manage the books. She was so scandalous! Walking through the door, she was oriented: "There are large sums of money moving to and from, and it's difficult to keep accurate numbers." A bell went off! "If they can't notice this is a bird's nest on the ground." What made it easy to steal money from Blunt and his boys was his ridiculous infatuation; it never occurred to him to check the numbers she came up with at the end of the day!

But one day, it was discovered she had been skimming her cream right off the top, considering the enormous decline in numbers. Once a stable clientele was in place, the numbers usually panned out close from day to day unless new clients were picked up.

The two brothers both looked at Blunt.

"Blunt: Man, I know you don't think Janice is stealing."

They didn't say anything at first, thinking "she tapped the till; it's got to be that 'B' Janice!" So, they decided to lay back and pay closer attention to the product and cash flow. At the end of the day, they knew without a doubt she was the deceitful, unappreciative culprit; the penalty for such an act was punishable by "acid mutilation."

They would go to any extent necessary when punishment had to be executed; the goal was to send out an outrageous subliminal message and conjure the most despicable idea that emphasized "don't cross the boss!" Blunt paid a young kid, 15 years old, five hundred dollars with instructions to throw acid in her face! Blunt knew she loved her wings like Wendy Williams, so he gave the kid a description of what she looked like and the address where she lived, along with a bag of wigs.

"When she answers the door, tell her you have wigs for sale! The second she tries one of them on, dash the acid in her face and make the evidence disappear in the sewer system."

The youngster went to the location, geared up, knowing he was going to pass his initiation. As he drove by the house, missing the address, he saw a lady in the backyard, who happened to be Janice. He detoured quickly through the alley. He got out of the car and held a wig in his hand.

"Wigs for sale! Would you be interested?"

"Janice: Wait a minute, son. Let me see what you have. I like my wigs!"

He gave her the one he had in his hand to try on. The minute she occupied both her hands adjusting the wig, he dashed, throwing acid in her face and ran to his stolen car, hopped in, and sped off, peeling rubber.

She began frantically screaming until her 6-year-old daughter, Kendra, ran to the backyard to see why her mother was screaming. She noticed her mother holding her hands to her face but not quite touching it. Her face felt really hot! She held her mom tight while she screamed in tears and agony; unfortunately, Kendra also suffered minor acid burns from the residue inflicted.

"Kendra: Mommy, Mommy! I'm going in the house to dial 911."

The police department dispatched an ambulance service so that they would arrive at perhaps the same time; approaching her with delicacy, she was so fragile, with skin dripping from her face!

The police noticed a wig lying on the ground and picked it up to try and get DNA. The ambulance department hurried her into the vehicle to be transported to the emergency room! The police, under excruciating circumstances, refused to attempt questioning the victim at the scene because she was not only in a hysterical state, but she was also physically deficient! They did ask her 5-year-old child if she saw what happened to her mom. She responded, saying she knew nothing.

"The only thing I do know is my mother was screaming really loud, and I ran to her aid in the backyard to see why she was screaming. It wasn't until I ran to hug her that I found she was in unbearable pain and agony. I also discovered something had burned me in a few spots."

At that point, the police asked to see the minor burns on her arm. Stopping the ambulance before it could get en route, the police suggested they take her to the hospital as well because she had suffered burns on her arm.

The next day, the police went to the hospital to investigate the crime. The victim was calm from the pain medication administered.

"Officer Smith: How do you feel?"

"Janice: I'm much better today!"

"Officer Smith: Can I ask you some questions that may be helpful in capturing the perpetrator who did this to you?"

"Janice: Sure!"

"Officer Smith: Can you give me a description of this person?"

"Janice: He appeared to be about 15 years old, stood about 5'4", and wore jeans with a blue striped plaid shirt. He drove off in a blue Chevy Impala on 20-inch wheels. I couldn't help noticing he was so young."

"Officer Smith: Do you know anybody who would have something like this done to you?"

"The only thing I can tell you is some kids came down the alley while I was hanging towels on the line to dry! He got my attention with some wigs he said he was selling; I asked to try on the one that caught my eye. The minute I pulled it down onto my head, he threw acid in my face, jumped in a car, and fled, peeling rubber while laughing!"

"Officer: Is there anything else you can tell me?"

"Janice: No!"

"Officer: Well, here's my card. If anything should come to you that may be helpful, please give me a call!"

Chapter 33

Thirty minutes later, back at Pleasure Island Resort, Banks called the horse stable and told Cortez to send Mike and Jerry to his office after they finished riding. Twenty minutes later, galloping in the stable, Cortez reached out for the bridle on Mike's horse, telling him, "Mr. Banks would like to see the two of you in his office."

Dismounted, they took the saddles and bridles off the horses to hurry them back into their individual stalls. They walked Carol and Sherry across the huge plot of land back to Grandma's house.

Once they made it to the house, Jerry and Mike told them they had to go see Banks.

Walking into his office, Jerry greeted him, followed by the information received from Cortez.

"We were told you wanted to see us?"

"Banks: That's correct! I want you to know your grandma's lease is expired, and she has decided to buy the condo; this relinquishes any and all rights we may have had to enter her unit in the manner we have in the past! Therefore, what I need you to do is make yourselves available to trip the wires if we're denied access from the adjoining unit!"

"Mike: Yes, Sir! Just give us a call, and we'll be there within two hours. Will that be all?"

"Mr. Banks: Yes!"

Departing his office silently, walking out the door, Jerry put his index finger on his tongue, took it out, and said, "This is one on you, Banks… More evidence!"

They returned to get Carol and Sherry to go out for dinner at the nearest restaurant before heading home.

Early the next morning, Jerry called Dino and Little Rob to get the day started! Little Rob was an early bird. He was at the donut shop before the police, buying one dozen donuts and a gallon of milk for him and the boys; it was 7 AM, time for the addicts to get their breakfast, cocaine on the rocks!

They never slept! 24/7, they lurked around trying to find white specks on the floor, believing it was cocaine. Not only were they psychologically strung out on the drug, but they were also literally sick, living in an unrealistic world where everything revolved around crack! At 7 AM sharp, you could count on a knock at the door.

"Excited to get a medication refill that only lasted 5 minutes: Knock, knock!"

Little Rob answered, "What can I do for you, playboy?"

"Larry: Give me a fifty-cent piece of that apple pie, baby!"

Larry was served, and Tony followed suit.

"Give me a gram, so I can make it sizzle like bacon."

"Rob: That's what I call a wake-up call. You're going to blow your brains out!"

"Larry: Man, you know this only gets rid of the 'hanks'! It cranks my engine to get me geared up to get some money," he said, talking to himself as he walked down the street.

"You ought to be blessed, brother. I spend all my money with you," he said, walking down the street, trying to find a gallery!

Neither of them had a straight shooter and couldn't find a car to break one off.

"Larry: Let's go to Pete's smoking gallery!"

The smoking gallery happened to be an abandoned building that dope fiend Pete assumed full ownership of.

"Tony: Forget that! I'm not going. All they want to do is hang over your shoulder and beg for a hit to use a straight shooter and a room; classic straight shooters made out of glass tubes, antennas, light bulbs, and the like! They have nothing better to do."

Pete wanted his hit for the use of "his abandoned building with amenities." He opened a shop that advocated tuberculosis, hepatitis B & C, and AIDS all wrapped together.

"Who died and made him boss!"

All that no-good low-down son of a gun knew was how to beg for a hit; he got food stamps from the government and donations from the neighborhood food pantries and churches!

Larry interrupted, "Man, come on! You know how to say no if you don't like my energy! Besides, 'G', you act like you never begged for a hit from time to time."

"Larry: You're right! Let's go!"

Once they arrived at this disgusting abandoned building, with couches in the living room sitting on bricks to elevate them off the floor, the word "condemned" was written on the red-colored boards!

To him, that only meant the government was protecting his property from vandalism. Users normally snuck in and out to avoid the wrong people observing them enter the building.

Pete really had this abandoned building wired. He took several car batteries and wired them to everything imaginable. He ran wires from car batteries to headlights he'd stolen off cars to light the unit. He would strip wires from the backs of televisions, connect two adjoining wires, and run them directly to the battery to gain the basic channels. But he would stop there; he knew a guy who would shimmy up the pole and circumvent the wires to access cable TV.

He had hot plates, small refrigerators, microwave ovens! Batteries were essential to Pete's creational home; there was, of course, no water in the building. They would use water that remained in the back of the urinal and send runners out to the nearby school to secure buckets of water for washing and making hot water for cooking!

He had a coffee table in the center of the floor propped on milk crates used as leg replacements! In the master bedroom, on the floor, was an old, worn-out mattress, a lantern lamp operated by kerosene, a headlight from a car, a space heater, and a toilet filled with defecation, and a sink you didn't want to touch.

For entertainment at Pete's, you watched addicts slither on the floor trying to find a hit. He could see where the term "sun porch" derived from; you could see daylight through the boards! The windows were all broken out and replaced with boards. Being lit by 12-volt batteries was a lifestyle!

But when the power failed, their reserve kicked in; innate visions like bats and rats roamed in the night with infrared assistance!

The backup lights were kerosene lamps. You might want to put a new alarm system on your car to prevent a battery disappearance; as you entered the door, you were greeted as though you had walked into a rehab clinic!

A drug addict's convention with a two-pronged program: load and fire! They were nowhere near the twelve-step program; it must be that dilemma of "giving up the good feeling for the bad!"

"Pete: What you got for me?"

They both chipped a piece off their rock, looking at one another as Pete boarded the front door to prevent a draft and someone from walking in unannounced!

He had to get his hit. After they finally made it to the top of the stairs, the normal response was to look around to see who they knew. The first familiar face was Sylvester, who happened to be a brilliant columnist for the New York Daily Tribune, getting high before work; Charlie, security for Boatman's Bank; and Barbara, a registered nurse who carried a purse filled with pills she shoplifted from her job.

The one drug she couldn't manage to get was crack! The neighborhood taxi cab driver Harmon was always short with the company's money because he knew he could make the money back before turning it in; the twin sisters Alley and Alice stopped by daily to hit that glass pipe!

Larry asked to use Alley's straight shooter, and she said, "Treat me like the house and hand me a utility knife."

Without hesitation, he cut her off a small piece.

"She looks at him and says, 'Is this the best you can do for a sister?'"

He pinched off another piece.

"Okay then! This is much better! Treat a bitch right, and she'll treat you right! Can we get that beautiful understanding? And don't hit my shooter too hard either. You brothers don't know how to hit it right! Mess my stuff up!"

Tony asked to use Jimmy's straight shooter.

"Jimmy: Sure, you can use it if you give me a bump!"

Before Tony could agree to give him a bump, he pulled out a razor knife and attempted to cut a piece off Tony's dope lying on the table.

"Tony: Wait a minute! You don't just take what you want. I'll give you what I want you to have. Better yet! Pete! Let me out of this crazy house."

Larry noticed Tony having problems, so he stepped in to see what had happened.

"Tony: Man, this stupid fool thinks he can cut off a piece of my stuff to use his shooter," he explained while sifting through the trash, trying to find a soda can to poke holes in, a piece of steel wool, and a "pusher" to pack the smoking apparatus; to no avail! He really didn't want to give Jimmy any of his dope.

"Tony: Pete, let me out so I can find a can to hook my stuff up."

He walked for nearly a block before finding a can and a small Jack Daniel's bottle! Hurriedly, he went back to the gallery, knowing there was no problem getting the other essentials to manufacture his straight shooter!

Before Sylvester the columnist exited the party, he said, "I have two complimentary box seat tickets to a live play! A hit can get you two tickets. If you know someone interested, I'll be back provided they're not sold."

Using cocaine and heroin created unimaginable euphoric body orgasms that made you take grave risks with your life and employment!

As you could transparently see here, with the promising editor, the nurse; people like Bobby Brown and Whitney Houston had paid visits to the gallery!

Chapter 34

Phantom the millions of addicts who have absolutely no control, submissive to a drug they are powerless against. Tucked in abandoned buildings in communities across the nation, they fight off infections while engaging without restrictions in a game of Russian roulette that could zap their lives in a second, unconsciously confronting diseases that have no name or face!

Those germs and diseases roamed rampantly like termites. The kids weren't immunized from this indiscriminate precipitation; imagine bi-state and school bus drivers stopping by prior to picking up the children for school!

Addicts stopping by, leaving their kids in one room while they smoked in another! Pete was a smart dumb brother. He knew how to get lights and water; how to get food stamps!

He knew where all the local food pantries were and all the best places to get batteries recharged without question: Auto Zone, O'Reilly's, "Advance Auto," and shade tree mechanics. It made you wonder why kids came to school in a daze, couldn't comprehend quickly, and moved like zombies, with attitudes wearing nasty, smelly kerosene scents!

What an absurd place to live! Anyway, later that evening, the narcotics squad kicked in Blunt's dope house for drugs. Eight police officers stormed up the steps with a battering ram, thrashing the door open. Blunt's boys noticed the movement and started cleaning up. The drugs were quickly poured into a bucket of acid for disposal; Little Clyde leaped out the second-floor window!

He landed quite hard, fracturing his pelvis; he didn't notice the fracture from the excitement and adrenaline rush that forcefully propelled him to run faster to get away!

That was his only concern at that time. Blunt and Dexter went to jail for possession of firearms and an unexplainable 25 thousand dollars hidden in the ceiling tile; they didn't arrest them on sales charges because they couldn't determine who sold the drugs.

That evening, they were both released from custody on bail! Their bonds were set at 25 thousand dollars. Blunt and Dexter walked out of jail laughing.

"Blunt: At least we had the opportunity to get rid of the stuff. Now we have to acquire an attorney that specializes in this kind of case. We're in it to win it!"

"Dexter: It's only paper, and we got plenty. I wonder what happened to Little Clyde. I saw him jump out the back window."

Two days later, Clyde called Do Good on his cell. He told him he didn't know what the outcome was, but "scat" kicked in and caught Blunt and Dexter.

"I jumped out the back window and fractured my pelvis bone. I'm in the hospital right now; I can't get out of bed. The doctor said it'll take about 16 weeks before a full recovery is procured."

"Do Good: It's great to hear you'll be okay. Dino and I went to post bail for Blunt and Dexter. I want to visit, but the man might have his watchdogs planted at the hospital. If you need anything, just hit me on my horn and I'll make sure you get it."

"Clyde: Okay!"

"Do Good: Hang in there! It's going to be alright, my brother. Oh! Before you get out of there, we will have to find another spot."

"Clyde: I knew you were going to say that. Very smart!"

"Do Good: I'm out! I'll chat with you later!"

"Do Good" told Dino what had happened to Clyde.

"Dino: The brother is strong! But I don't understand how he was able to move with a fractured pelvis? Do Good: I hope you're okay. Who's the bad blood connection?"

Let me call Mike and Jerry to inform them so they'll know we had to get rid of the drugs in the acid pan and the money was confiscated as evidence!

Do Good made the call to Mike to inform him what had happened. The phone rang, and Mike picked up.

"Do Good: The police kicked in, but they didn't get any drugs. They took 15 thousand dollars and two guns! Clyde managed to get away, jumping out the back window, which landed him in the hospital with a fractured pelvis."

"Mike: I'm glad you got with us ASAP so we could pass the word: we have a malfunction in the organization! I'll get back with you guys later."

It was discovered the guy Dino hit with his gun, knocking him down the flight of stairs, got caught with two rocks! He probably did a quid pro quo with the police for his release, or it could have been Janice who got dashed with the acid. Ironically, the police also had Throw Down's apartment on the east side under surveillance.

Fast Eddie or Janice told them about Throw Down's spot as well.

The informant went crazy "painting" for the narcotics squad? Their house of cards was imploding by the hour; the hourglass wasn't sparing one second; their foundation was decaying!

Lt. Frank Lewinski from narcotics went to the judge with an application for a search warrant that tendered information obtained by the C.I. Lt. Frank came out of the judge's chambers and kissed the warrant.

"We got his behind now," he said. "I told those thunders to stay out of my district with their drugs, destroying lives and terrorizing my community!"

Throw Down, in the meantime, had been lying up in a hotel for three hours with his girlfriend; the police had absolutely no way of knowing who was on the other side of the door!

Traffic was high volume with no end. People were repetitively going in and out of the unit, deciding now was the time to take them down. The judge allowed thirty days in which to execute the warrant before its expiration; the timing was right! It was now or never! Two officers rushed to the rear of the apartment to prevent any possible escapes, while the other six officers, all dressed in bulletproof vests, prepared for any altercation that might occur when they kicked in the front entrance.

The police announced their code "flash" over the radio, and at that time, all the officers thrust forward in their mission to bring these guys down! Just as they hit the door the first time without announcement, Stan didn't know what to think. He had been given rigid instructions: "If anything out of the norm happens, dispose of the dope in the bucket of acid." M-1 didn't know what to think either, especially since there wasn't a police announcement! He thought it was some dumb fool tired of living trying to rob them and commit suicide because the police department didn't move like that.

He fired through the door. At the same time, the door flew open. To his surprise, standing on the other side was a bunch of police wearing masks, all pointing guns directly at him. The first shot fired hit him in the chest, knocking him to the floor. M-1 was rushed to the hospital, where he was later charged with unlawfully discharging a firearm, armed criminal action, attempted assault on a police officer, and possession of a firearm! His partner Stan was charged with possession of a firearm and armed criminal action; he was also charged with possession of cocaine and marijuana. When he threw the cocaine in the acid, some of the residue settled on the rim of the bucket. He didn't have time to clean up the mess. When you panic, things happen; "Is it really worth it?"

Stan's bond was set at 35 thousand dollars. Ervin Wells (AKA M-1) had his bond set at 75 thousand dollars. Throw Down made it back to the apartment four hours later to find the police had kicked in.

An addict standing on the corner noticed Throw Down's car and jogged down the street to tell him what had happened. "About ten undercover cops kicked in, and M-1 got shot." He knew Throw Down would give him a bump for his information. Throw Down told the guy, "I'm ill-prepared right now, playa, but I'll catch you later and bless you for this information." He hopped in his car and sped off from the apartment! He assumed the bust was intended for him, considering he was the management at that location. He was excited; he decided to take his lady to the hotel to spend quality time treating their sexual appetites equitably! Nature called!

Afterwards, while driving, he contemplated the reason this was suddenly happening. He reflected back to the guy he kicked down the stairs, the girl who got burned with acid, and all the other incidents that had occurred. With that, he decided to call Dino and Do Good to suggest they close down shop for at least a week to clear the air and relocate.

"Do Good" interrupted, "Let me get back with you on this."

"Throw Down: Talk to you!"

Do Good hung up and called Mike and Jerry to inform them the situation was worsening. Throw Down's people had just got caught, and M-1 was shot in the chest by the police! The police took 15 thousand in cash from that spot. They were extremely lucky to get a chance to drop the dope in the acid because everything happened incredibly fast.

"I think we should shut down for a month instead of a week or two."

Jerry paused, thinking about how Banks was going to respond to their situation.

"Mike: Yeah! Why not! Let's shut down until further notice. I'll call my guy and explain how things are spiraling out of control; two houses were kicked in, and Throw Down was shot while Clyde fractured his pelvis bone lying in the hospital!"

Mike called Mr. Banks and explained what had happened.

"Banks: How much damage did we sustain?"

"Mike: 40 thousand in revenue and approximately 30 thousand in product; it was dumped in the acid before they could get into the apartment."

"Banks: Question! Were any of your people employed legally?"

"Mike: No! Strictly street hustlers."

"Banks: I guess we'll have to eat the loss because neither of you can contest without someone in your camp having employment!"

Throw Down insisted it was Fast Eddie, and something had to be done to make addicts think before telling the police; they needed to make a classic example out of Fast Eddie like yesterday! At least they would know he wouldn't be able to testify when motions were filed to produce the identification of the unreliable confidential informant, who probably made the deal in exchange for his freedom; an informant would lie on anybody to save his own hide!

In that moment, Throw Down bought "deacon rat poison" and told Dino what his intentions were.

"Dino: Do you know where to catch the guy?"

"Throw Down: That's not a problem! The streets have very sensitive ears, walls have ears, and windows have eyes. These dope fiends are swift, extreme opportunists and will do practically anything to go see Scottie! If the poison doesn't work, we can always revert to loading him up with heroin and treat it like an overdose."

Dino and Do Good went to get Throw Down in Dino's black BMW.

They went to "Schnucks" store to buy some rat poison and a ten-day supply of diabetic syringes. Dino carried a Tec 9, and Throw Down had a .45 automatic; Do Good had a .38 special. Riding from sunup till sundown, they were about ready to turn in from exhaustion and empty stomachs! They had literally forgotten to eat because they could only see one thing: the whites of Fast Eddie's eyes; this was their lucky day!

Guess who was at the red light intersection crossing the street? Fast Eddie at 10 o'clock. The streets seemed like a ghost town. Deserted! This was the right time to grab him and throw him in the trunk of the car.

Dino and Throw Down jumped out of the car, forcing him into the trunk by gunpoint! Before the trunk was completely shut, the shock and panic propelled him to kick the trunk back open, yelling, "Help! Help! Wait a minute! What is this all about?" The trunk closed, muffling his voice. Taking him to an old abandoned building, down in the basement, they tied his hands to an overhanging galvanized pipe. Throw Down found a dirty rag lying on the filthy floor and stuffed it in his mouth to prevent screaming. Anxious to get him inside without being noticed, they forgot to get the rat poison.

Do Good tossed Throw Down the keys, and he ran back to the car to get the poison, heroin, and syringe, plus a top to mix it. Before administering the poison, they beat him severely, rendering him almost in an unconscious state. Throw Down crushed the poison in a jelly jar top and got a trickle of water from a leaky pipe to convert the poison into a liquid form so it could be drawn up in the syringe!

He then asked Dino and Do Good if they had a cigarette he could use the filter to draw the solution into the syringe; they both replied no!

Throw Down, looking around on the floor, found a cigarette butt. He put it in the top and began drawing it up to shoot it into his vein; it didn't seem to work right away, so he drew again to give him a second dose! This time it worked, but they wanted to hang around to be sure he was dead before leaving. Dino slapped Fast Eddie to see if he was dead. He uttered a sound, so they filled the syringe with more heroin; only this time they left him for dead! For sure!

The police discovered him a week later by a strong stench coming from the old building! A passerby went in to find a straight shooter and smelled a peculiar odor that smelled like a dead body. As he continued to walk through this dark basement, he saw Fast Eddie hanging from a pipe. He immediately contacted the police department.

The police finally arrived, going into the basement to find Fast Eddie hanging from a pipe, dead, with a dead rat hanging out of his mouth; the police department held a meeting after learning this. It was suggested that all abandoned buildings be boarded up with signs that read "All trespassers will be arrested and charged with trespassing and vagrancy!"

While riding through the neighborhood, no one said anything. Finally, Throw Down broke the ice, "I told that snitch that the next time he did something scandalous, they would find him in a trash can." Dino and Do Good didn't respond right away! They were in contemplation, wondering if they had left any traces of evidence behind.

Common sense says they were going to pursue this case vigorously because it was so brutal and diabolically executed; this was an obvious statement: "snitch!" Mike and Jerry had to make Stan and Ervin Wells' bond, but they wanted to remain anonymous, so they gave the money to their moms to contact a lawyer and bail bondsman.

"Jerry said to Mike, 15 thousand in cash is not a drop in the bucket. But it could have been much worse; Dino and Do Good had 3 keys, and their palms were itching with an irresistible enticing rash to get the ball rolling!"

So they encouraged Throw Down to get three young girls he knew to rent apartments on the north, east, south, and west sides of town to set up shop, keeping in mind the importance of being far away from the previous locations!

Chapter 35

A week later, everything was back on track. They rented three apartments in inconspicuous places; this time they bought three police scanners to get a better warning signal when the cops were on the prowl! They put a cop payroll to get better reception at all times. The monitors were watching nonstop with surround camera surveillance 24/7. But they were still playing a dangerous game of Russian roulette.

Dino was under surveillance. The ATF followed every move he made. They wanted to catch him with his underwear down once and for all. Dino kept it one hundred!

Do Good met with Blunt, Throw Down, and Little Rob in a clandestine place on the outskirts of New York; Do Good gave each of them five ounces. He didn't want to put out too much of what was going on, but money had to continue to move. He had to take the risk to live up to his resume that only read "Gambler!" With little chat, they went their separate ways. The boys knew this was the time to pay close attention to their surroundings and keep their ears closer to the ground than groundhogs and fastened to the walls like termites at a marveling feast, huge enough to last a lifetime with no distraction; this was a critical period for them.

A common-sense rule is, "If you get caught, you hustle harder!" Everything intensifies to a point of desperation. The volume increases. You have to grease your attorney's palms to keep him happy, to continue getting continuances to string your case out as long as possible; each continuance could cost as much as one to two thousand dollars as a setback. It depends on your wallet and status! They knew getting caught with the smoking gun could mean a term in prison!

Although their only alternative was to call a technical foul, the police's failure to announce who they were rendered the search warrant invalid. The law was breached, which suggested their rights were violated. But how do you prove that? We know in most cases offenders plea bargain, not necessarily because clients are guilty of the crime charged, but to the contrary; they are afraid to confront a jury?

They knew how much time they faced if going to trial and striking out at bat! Of course, bluffing was good for a while, but when the end started to draw near, the tempo of mental frustration raced to no end. Thinking! "My life's riding the line. What's the easiest way out without incurring deep irreparable gashes impossible to heal?"

The first day the dope house opened for business, a young lady, Maggie, and her partner in crime, "Short Dog," stopped by to get a 16th. Short Dog bought it and gave it to Maggie to hide in case they were caught on radar and pulled over by the police; she had a much better hiding place! A male officer was not going there. From the time they made the purchase until they reached their destination, Short Dog watched her like a hawk.

When they didn't know where to go to smoke their crack, heroin, or the like, they often wandered aimlessly to Pete's place; Maggie really lured him there because she had a fetus.

She always met prominent people you wouldn't normally meet! Professional ballplayers on all levels, legal and street; actors like Robert Downey Jr. and Charlie Sheen, known for their risky business. The daredevils who did it all from "A to Z." Charlie's stun! He moved by the shift of the wind; you wouldn't believe how they blended in. One reason they stopped there was that no one expected to see a star. Plus, that was an opportunity to gain education on particular characteristics necessary when making a film; if ever caught in that predicament, that would certainly be the most appropriate alibi? "I'm preparing for a movie!"

Maggie was at the front door yelling for Pete; he acknowledged the call and hurried down the steps to let them in!

"Pete: Hey love! What's going on? How did things work out yesterday? You had that trick spinning like a top! I noticed you didn't come back."

"Maggie: That guy tried to screw my brains out for a bump; I had to pretend I was having a spasm in my back to get that fool off me!"

"Pete: I'm glad everything worked out okay."

"Short Dog, what's up? I haven't seen you in a minute; you haven't been locked up, have you?"

"Short Dog: I'm good! Just trying to get right."

"Pete: What you got for me?"

"Maggie: Wait till we get upstairs; our package is together."

Maggie and Short Dog continued up the steps while Pete, with zeal, boarded the doors! He didn't want to miss his hit. He knew once they made it to the top of the stairs, all the "cluckers" and rock stars would merge like clowns in a circus. Rushing up the steps, Pete's leg went through a rotten step that he knew so well.

"Pete yelled for help! He was stuck! Everyone heard him, but no one wanted to be the first to come to his assistance because they didn't want to part with their straight shooters packed with crack and risk someone taking it. The straight shooters were so hot, it reminded you of being burned by a hot iron or the eye on an electric stove; they couldn't put fire in their pockets!

Pete remained stuck in the hole until two very young "drug dealers," who hung out on occasion to sell small hits to keep themselves going with the change. Five, ten, fifteen, and twenty dollar hits and don't leave out the crumbs for three dollars. This was Pete's lucky day! The two youngsters, ages 14 and 15, came to his rescue.

The addicts all sat around talking about "that's good for his stupid ass. He tells us where the weak step is every damn day, but he steps right in it. Plus, he shouldn't be begging so damn much!

It makes folks hate you. I see why everybody hates Chris! He's always doing something to try and get an extra hit; you'll never see so many people in your life crawling on the floor like babies racing for crumbs that appear to be crack! Picking it up to discover it's a tiny piece of lint, cotton, or a white flaky element torn from a paper towel!

"Pete: Thanks, my young brothers! I really appreciate you guys helping me out of that hole…"

Chapter 36

"Kenny and Mark: "Old G, you know we got your back; besides, if something were to happen to you, we wouldn't have a place to hang out during school hours when the cops are roaming through the hood."

He threw up deuces!

"Pete: Right, deuces! Then act like deuces and ante up and give me a hit!"

"Mark: I got a hit for you, alright; I'll knock your behind back down in that hole and leave you for dead!"

"Pete: Is this the way you treat an Old 'G'?"

"Kenny: Is this the way you treat a 'BG'? I see what teachers mean when they say, 'I always say we are the food we eat.' That's true because you are definitely rubbing off on me. And you know this! Word!"

"Maggie steps in with her two cents: That's why both your dumb behinds should be at home or in school learning how to win instead of learning how to lose."

"Mark: That sounded genuine coming from you, and I appreciated the concern. Home was not really home because both our parents did the same thing you're doing right now!"

"Kenny: We may as well be in the streets. It was terribly hard to think in terms of doing the right thing when you were programmed wrong about what was right; that's just a peek into my window! I had much love for you, sister! You knew that! I really appreciated the outpouring of concern, but I had to do what I had to do to survive in this dangerous jungle. Now that's what I called navigating a ship without a sail!"

Mark told Kenny, "Imagine! No defined education is like a ship without a sail; directions are determined by the shift of the wind, showing we are moving without purpose. But she didn't have to call us stupid not knowing the circumstances. She had a pipe in her hand, getting high, and we were her suppliers! Come on, man; she had the nerve. She's stupid!"

Mark and Kenny were gullible, destitute, and deeply embedded in an encroaching situation where they knew no logical answers; with the devastating triple threat of having no desire to challenge doing the right thing! At that point, they were in it for the long haul, waiting to be inducted into a Hall of Fame—an award only given to street hustlers that signified, "You are officially a thug!"

"Pete: Thanks again, guys!" Pete humbled himself; that was how he got his fix. The customer's always right motto!

The old G went back to doing what he was doing before the board collapsed, bruising his leg. He found Maggie and Short Dog sitting at a table, smoking crack by candlelight; Pete's hit was lying on the table! He smiled as he stuffed it into his uniquely designed pipe, fit for the king of kings of all crack smokers.

Addicts could be very quirky at times and depressed in the same breath. You never knew where they were coming from. Maggie's hands were tough from handling the crack pipe; she could pick up a skillet filled with grease and chicken that had been frying for ten minutes without the use of a glove. That was what I called alligator skin! Imagine the consequences of that massage. A nightmare!

Sylvester, the columnist, put his crumbs on a small mirror that sat on a tiny end table. A guy recklessly walked past and accidentally knocked it to the floor. Sylvester didn't get belligerent at first, but his expression changed. "Dang, man," he said. "You need to watch where you're going when passing through in a dimly lit room."

The stranger said, "Sorry, man! I wish I could help you out, but I don't have anything right now. You want me to help you find yours?"

Sylvester hurried to say, "No! I'll be fine!" By this time, the old G made his way into Sylvester's area; he saw Sylvester on his knees. He knew he dropped something onto the floor! Immediately, he commenced crawling on his knees to see if he could perhaps find the crumbs before Sylvester could get to them.

Sylvester was getting more and more upset as he crawled, thinking, "Pete is just trying to help himself to my crumbs." The situation intensified the second he stood up; he kicked Pete square in the butt. Flat on the floor he went.

Pete looked back and asked, "What was that for?"

"Sylvester: Because you think you're being slick, sucking up my dope off this carpet like Stanley Steemer! I haven't found one piece, and you're crawling with one hand open and one closed. I know you found some! No problem, though, bro; I'm out!"

He didn't get belligerent; he just left the premises. On his way out, Pete walked behind him, fussing!

"Sylvester blurted out, 'You better get some business!'"

"Pete: If you ever kick me again, you will be my business! Somebody will be writing a column on your ass! 'Columnist on crack got whacked!'"

Sylvester didn't respond!

Boiling like a crockpot later that day, Sylvester reported the abandonment of a deplorable building infested with notorious drug addicts and paraphernalia to City Hall. A response came from the New York Daily Tribune's leading reporter; they had to act with urgency, sending a crew out to secure the abandoned building against intruders immediately! The poster signs read, "Condemned Building! Anyone caught trespassing will go to jail."

The city had to rip boards down to gain entrance and get people out of the building! They walked through wearing masks, only coming up for air when necessary to avoid inhaling the stench that hovered with a peculiar combination of fumes that could be anything from cocaine, heroin, pot, meth, ecstasy, stale food, and funk. The list continued with vials, syringes, and unimaginable straight shooters of various styles lying all over the floor as though they were décor. Disgusting apparatuses were used to engage in dangerous games of "Russian roulette."

Pete and his colorful friends left without incident. Once the building was boarded up for the third time, evicting Pete, he realized now the city was serious about keeping him out of the abandoned building, so he decided to burn it to ashes. He went ballistic, going to the nearby service station to purchase one dollar's worth of gasoline;

that was all she wrote. The fire department rushed to the scene of a three-alarm fire but didn't make it in time to save the old crumbling, decayed building that should have been demolished years ago.

Pete's gut told him the reporter had something to do with the government boarding up his home; Pete's house was up in smoke! Pete disappeared from the neighborhood!

A month later, Mike and Jerry were still struggling with dope houses, bouncing from one location to another, reinventing and constantly rebuilding clientele; it was rough with all the confidential informants slamming people! They popped up all over the place; a brother couldn't breathe! Mike and Jerry started moving product solo to different spots so it wouldn't create any unnecessary buzz; they had come too far to fall now! Losing wasn't in the equation!

Mike and Jerry had to pay Banks a visit because they'd run out of the product. The Henson brothers were on the ball. They made things happen. They were right about Fast Eddie; since he had been out of the way, the vibe on the street was calm but still scary because when things seemed at peace, there was a volcano about to erupt somewhere! That didn't stop the move; though, it did cause a pause for caution at every intersection to look both ways before crossing; anything was possible! You might get hit by guess who was coming for dinner; Eugene Phillips!

Chapter 37

He was released from custody that day. The prosecuting attorney begrudgingly released him! They couldn't establish a legal foundation in which to present only weak circumstantial evidence to a jury! No eyewitnesses, no fingerprints, no DNA; the only strain of evidence secured was a man with one arm cut off at the elbow! The police department was encouraged to contact the news media at once to inform nationwide viewers that the alleged suspect accused of being the red light machete bandit had just been released from custody with the premise that the courts had insufficient evidence to support their claim against him; an immediate release was ordered!

His attorney's opinion was that he believed his client was innocent based on the evidence presented, but he was a defense attorney. He reluctantly congratulated him as he made his departure from the court building! The tempo of Eugene's heart started to race incredibly fast as he ran down the steps from the court building.

Callers who saw the news air immediately called in to try to rebuttal his release, but to no avail. The public outcry wasn't enough to keep him held in custody unjustly. Back to square one! A shock that grabbed the state of New York by the jugular again because this suspected maniac had unfortunately found his way back into the mainstream through technicalities; an eclipse of Lucifer had just re-emerged, creating uncertainty that covered the entire state with a blanket that spelled catastrophe, with yet another overwhelming blow from "the red light machete bandit's horribly terrifying story" that continued to haunt America.

Eugene knew his release was inevitable, reading all the road signs. The court couldn't hold a man with no evidence. He was blessed, and someone was cursed at the same time. Seconds after he was released from custody, church bells sounded! New York started praying! Everyone began rolling up windows! Gossip ran rampant everywhere: "The red light machete bandit was released!"

Eugene was critically processing his release; he knew it wouldn't be smart to get out and right away pick up where he left off, so he indecisively decided to back off for a while, especially since he was clear of drugs and alcohol! He just had recess! That wasn't his bottom; that was a "fox" hole prayer sales pitch! He still had more floors to go. A return was inevitable!

Larry was the most! Visiting places that enticed triggers to resurface. But for now, Eugene quietly crawled into an ant hole, his natural habitat for a while (prison). He knew from vibes everyone suspected him to continue; sometimes life handed you a bitter pill and forced it down your throat!

While Eugene enjoyed his first breath of fresh air after 45 days spent in jail, oops! He got an itch! He couldn't resist the lifestyle. He made his way to his friend's house to pick up his gear: a machete and holster. He couldn't wait till nightfall to leap out on a dope dealer. He knew he couldn't get out of the game with all of the arms he had cut off. Eugene acquired a mental disorder after the loss of his arm. He achieved a euphoria that changed his demeanor, depicting a fox chasing his prey.

The red light machete bandit was on the prowl again. He had three vices: alcohol, drugs, and an appetite for dope dealers' jewelry to take back to another dealer in exchange for dope. A career criminal was on the loose. He didn't move until nightfall. On this particular night, he decided to hang around "Club Boss."

Two boss dope dealers pulled into the parking lot. Mr. Diamond Tip and his lady friend, Starlight, draped in diamonds, emerged from an electric Elon Musk Tesla Roadster special edition. Right then, he knew that was his dinner for the evening. He waited outside like a snake lying in the grass till late night; finally, he saw them walking down the steps, leaving the club, laughing and precariously staggering as they walked.

Starlight was on the driver's side. Mr. Tip was too tipsy; he went to the passenger's side because he was too inebriated to drive. She rolled down the window to light a cigarette, and at that precise time, he crept his way to the car, kneeling down below the back passenger's side on the driver's side so she couldn't see him through her side mirror.

The second she thumped the ash out the window, the machete thrust down on her hand with tremendous impact; her hand fell to the ground. The bandit grabbed the hand, quickly snatching off the jewelry, and suddenly disappeared into the forest. At that moment, Tip woke up from his incoherence to realize his lady just lost her hand.

In a panic, he reached for a rag as she continued screaming and waving her arm back and forth until he caught it and wrapped it to slow the blood flow so he could call for help. He dialed 911.

The ambulance and the police arrived. They found her hand and rushed her to the hospital immediately. The police hung around asking questions. That same evening, the news reported a lady's hand was cut off at "Club Boss," and the perpetrator faded into the forest. No one was able to identify this person, but we have reason to believe the Red Light Machete Bandit is back. It is important to note that this is serious, and you need to proceed with caution while driving.

Two days later, the Red Light Machete Bandit's two habits were kicking in simultaneously: his alcohol and drugs, both being physical addictions that caused pain when you could not get them. He went to the liquor store to buy something to drink to ease the pain. He was lucky. He just saw his next victim.

His sign of attack: he started to drool uncontrollably until he caught his prey. He couldn't resist a flashy dope dealer mad at his woman, talking angrily to himself and not focused; an act of desperation! He caught him in the lot and whacked his hand off, pointing the machete at his victim, threatening to cut him as he picked up the hand to take the jewelry.

He had a mask and hooded sweater on; that was the norm due to the COVID virus. The liquor store camera could only reveal to the police a masked man with a machete savoring the man's hand and disappearing from the scene, running east.

The news media reported that day that the Red Light Machete Bandit was on another one of his rampages; we must be vigilant. He had the entire state of New York, all branches state and federal, on the hunt while citizens sat in fear.

Mike and Jerry, on the other hand, were clinically a nervous wreck, being extorted to harbor bombs that could explode at any second. That constantly kept them stressed, contemplating that their ultimate demise would be Banks was going to kill them in the end; they'd come to know too much!

Banks was smart! He attended Yale College, mastering in psychology and minoring in business, which enabled him to become a renowned guru in both fields; he was the best in the business!

Chapter 38

Mike and Jerry had to be very careful about what they said; those devices were alive and well. They knew they were being monitored and wanted to sucker him up with their respect for him regardless of how he played them. They still had to honor and respect the game, especially on his level.

"Mike: Mr. Banks is suave, cunning, and an amazingly insidious guy who has a peculiar, eminent air that weirdly suggests death. He has us by the hand. But I can also see a picture of hope. The boys, were we way out of our league this time… Speaking success into existence; we will win in the end. Looking at the glass half full!"

"Jerry: Mr. Banks is a master. His name should have been Mr. A.I. He's professionally crude and absurd, has incredible business savvy; he's straightforward and stands by his word. On the outside looking in, I find the guy very intriguingly impressive as though he was picture-perfect. However, he's dangerous… I am intrigued by how his strategic mind works. He reminds me of Donald Trump; you don't like some of the things he does, but he's straightforward; he's a boss."

"Hopefully, it's that time he is going to dismantle the device inside of us; he can only say yes or no!" Mike paused for a second to collect himself. "This lifestyle is sucking the life out of me; sure, I wear a professional smile, appearing as though I'm living this perfect life of a successful entrepreneur! But if the badly butchered interior were turned inside out, you'd clearly see the naked truth; a gross open wound with boiling hot blood like lava pouring down the inner seams, causing stress and depression to intertwine together like an insane exhibitionist strapped and compressed inside a box with no ventilation! Desperately trying to endure the pain by reluctantly kneeling before his feet to appease his inflamed appetite to play this crazy game of risk, using us as the unmerciful risk-takers!"

After driving 45 minutes and pulling onto the estate, they greeted the gatekeeper to get in. Slowly, the gate opened as they entered "Banks' Wonderland," going to see the wizard. His secretary called into his office, telling him they had arrived.

"Banks: Send them right in! How's it going, fellows?" Mike spoke to himself: We've committed well over 30 criminal offenses from selling drugs to trafficking weapons, to blowing up warehouses with mob bosses inside arguing over spilled blood that found no compromise. Blowing up cars and killing innocent people who only wanted a ride home; killing people in hotels and other unthinkable venues!

He had us walk into a gambling casino to meet with an employee who transported the money to the vault and signed out monies transported to the bank; the plan was "two masked men sneak into the office area, wearing masks and catch the transporter with the money!" He was easily persuaded by gunpoint to hand over the money; it was all captured on camera, and his voice was incapacitated!

"Jerry spoke: Everything's going well! How about yourself?"

"Banks: I'm well! Thanks! Have a seat."

"Mike: Yes, sir!" Mike was still choked up a bit but improvised well!

"Banks: When was the last time you guys had a relaxed moment? I can see the tenacious mindset! You stay on the go! I'll tell you what! I'm inviting the two of you and your companions to a night out to be well entertained."

Mike and Jerry were both "TKO'd" by the best! He had gone so far left field; they were outdone!

"Jerry: It's been a long time since we've had an opportunity to enjoy ourselves without some type of restraint."

"Banks: I get what you're hinting at. I've got to be quite honest with you; you stole from me, and your debt hasn't been paid, but I'm a gentleman. Instead of killing you and strapping cement boots on your feet and dropping you in the river, I employed the two of you, making really good salaries with fringe benefits to manage my business with fringe benefits like this." He handed them ten passes for their friends as well!

"Banks: To fill in the missing blanks, this is our annual treat to all stockholders, family, and friends because we are family and friends in a business that has been phenomenally rewarding; featuring Kenny G, Toni Braxton, Randy Travis, and Nicki Minaj!"

The food, alcoholic beverages, and soft drinks were free. It would be an evening to remember! "Be sure to bring your ladies," Banks said.

Mike asked, "When is the event?"

"I'm sorry, guys. It's next Saturday," Banks replied, and they both accepted the invite with broad smiles, shaking his hand.

"Oh, I did forget to mention the time and date! I apologize! It's next Saturday from 7:00 PM till 11:00 PM!" Banks added. The last piece of business came when he handed them six keys of cocaine in two briefcases.

"Thanks, Mr. Banks!" Mike said.

"Thanks, Mr. Banks!" Jerry echoed. Walking out the door, they looked at one another but couldn't say anything.

Once they left the estate, the texting commenced, going back and forth discussing a possible plan to get all their boys in to case the joint out just in case they had to come in the back door on Banks to bring down his house built on sand. The event was scheduled to be held in an indoor pool area that accommodated 500 guests; they were also allowed to roam freely on the grounds.

"This may be our once-in-a-lifetime opportunity," Mike said to Jerry. "We have to take full advantage of every opportunity afforded to us."

"We can invite Dino, Do Good, their girlfriends, and four of our boys, like Throw Down and Blunt, for instance," Jerry suggested. "The plan is to slip out of the crowd during the peak of the concert and explore every discreet option possible to sneak back onto the property without the gatekeeper's knowledge! Cameras may be an issue, so we must be extremely careful."

When they made it back to the city, they went straight to Dino and Do Good's home, gave them a package, and collected their cash.

Mike told Dino and his brother, "We need you guys to attend this event coming up next Saturday at Pleasure Island Resort; this is our connection, and you need to know this because if anything should happen to us, you'll know the conduit responsible! Plus, we want to show you something that'll blow your mind. The event is going to be really good with Kenny G, Tim McGraw, Toni Braxton, and Nicki Minaj."

Dino exclaimed, "That's gangster! But who is Tim McGraw?"

"He's a country singer!" Mike replied.

The day before the event, Mike made sure Carol's mini recorder was working properly to collect essential data to be used as evidence to gain leverage to escape the clutches of Banks at 3:00 PM Saturday that evening!

Dino and Martha rode with Do Good and Ebony! Mike, Sherry, and Carol rode with Mike! Throw Down and his boys rode together in the third vehicle, choking on chronic and laughing the entire time; Ebony was so excited getting out of rehab. She hadn't seen Do Good in two weeks. She talked the entire time while en route to the concert; when they got there, Samantha and 15 of her girls flew in from Florida, following them through the gate in two blue limousines with "Samantha/Wiggins" written on the side in fancy print.

When they got out of the limo, they stopped traffic, wearing their scandalous tiny party outfits, serving the guests with unprecedented four-star royal treatment.

Wiggins and Samantha gracefully made their entrance known as co-owners of the very prominently successful Boatman and

Mercantile banks, owners of volumes of extraordinary businesses such as expensive real estate from coast to coast. They aimed to merge together in a joint venture to construct a 21st-century state-of-the-art luxuriously fascinating facility that earmarked a remarkable escort service for stars on the down-low who took the risk of playing the game in the outfield to secure success!

At that intense interruption, there was a distraction; they were willing to gamble by sampling the eye candy, the forbidden fruit that could easily destroy the rest of their lives and careers. They knew if the fruit tasted good, they would taste it for a second time! Then the uncontrollable addiction kicked in, and the appetite subconsciously begged to sample other fruit until they had sampled every delicious fruit on display in the window; it was contagious! "Ask Charlie!"

Chapter 39

Attending the yearly event, a few celebrities on the marquee of acknowledgments included: Mrs. Rita McDowell, secretary for the United States Supreme Court; Calvin McCoy, Chief of Police in Washington, DC; State Senators from eight different states; all stakeholders of the resort chain from coast to coast, which made one wonder who was involved in Banks' elaborate scheme to establish drug rings extending coast to coast in many neighboring cities. Banks was the CEO with exclusive control in all the sister states! He and Starlet Templeton, his private investigator, had become an item. Their relationship was tightly knitted since his wife passed.

Mike, Carol, Jerry, and Sherry discussed seating arrangements necessary to identify the key players in the cartel. The general rule was that the elite always acquired the best seats. So the plan was to navigate their way through the pool area to get pictures of the arrangement.

Walking through the doors, they were blown away by the landscaped white pillows in each corner to support the structure. The seating arrangement was exceptional, spacious, with never-before-seen marble-top tables adorned with Mark Angelo's paintings imprinted, and very eloquently designed chairs that made one feel like a prince or princess! Out of the one hundred tables, only five tables were reserved.

"Bingo!" Carol exclaimed.

They knew to sit in the very next row behind the special guests. Mike, Carol, Jerry, and Sherry sat together. Carol's responsibility was to capture conversations and pictures whenever possible to establish the roles played in the relationship with Banks; the motto was "careful is not careful enough!" This was a very delicate situation. Getting caught could be imminent; they couldn't afford the price tag attached to fumbling the egg.

Imagine riding down a rocky slope traveling 60 miles an hour juggling one dozen eggs like a clown with the stipulation "if one cracks, you die!" All they could do was strap themselves in tight. The Henson brothers and their ladies sat at a table next to them in anticipation. Throw Down and his boys enjoyed a table in the next section with a good visual of each other. While everyone was being seated, the sounds of jazz fusion played. The waitresses were determined to keep everyone happy; they floated through the crowd like experts, on automatic pilot—nonstop!

"Do Good" and Ebony talked almost the entire time, getting reacquainted, revitalizing their relationship; she was doing really well this time. She was looking to the stars with plans to get back into modeling from a sober, humble perspective and be incredibly productive.

During their conversation, Toni Braxton and her three sisters—Trina, Tamar, and Towanda—pulled onto the estate in a white limousine that bore the signature marks "Toni Braxton"! Toni wore a soft peach-colored Donna Karan sheer silk dress with a low-cut revealing design that clearly showcased her cleavage; it was cut at a ridiculously short length, creating an amazing sassy look! She certainly didn't want to disappoint; her sexy swag was magnetic!

The guests were now all seated. Fifty-four-star waitresses took orders to be served at the tables. Of course, it came with a price, which didn't matter to them because the show was absolutely amazing. All the guests poured gratitude and excitement into paying homage for the invites!

Carol commenced snapping shots once the special guests arrived. Banks and Starlet made their way over to Wiggins and the other guests seated at the reserved tables. Carol flashed her camera with a "Madea" attitude to get revenge; Carol's vendetta against Robert Banks was to the core! Mike or Jerry could never imagine to what extent she and Sherry were willing to go; they would soon find out!

Mike and Sherry's grandmother didn't attend the gala event, but she said she heard the sweet sounds of Kenny G's horn whispering through her window and the eloquent sounds of Mrs. Toni Braxton! She didn't distinguish the other artists, but they came across well.

The show started with the dimming of the lights. Mike and Jerry got Dino, Do Good, and Throw Down's attention, then beckoned them to exit the pool area. Mike had a small camera hidden inside his tie clamp; he provided them with infrared scope glasses used as pathfinders to maintain a good visual at night; using flashlights wouldn't be smart.

If light deflected off a sign or something, it could be disastrous; they were on a mass witch hunt, vigilantly scouring the estate, leaving no stones unturned. Desperately searching to find a breach in security to get back on the premises unnoticed; time certainly wasn't their friend! According to the itinerary, it mentioned the program would start at 7:00 PM and end at 11:00 PM; therefore, time was of the essence.

"Throw Down, calm down, guys! We need to quit playing and stay focused; I want to get back to the concert. Plus, I am not a Green Beret; this woods stuff is for the birds! Does he traffic guns too? He's definitely a heavyweight!"

"He's heavier than you can imagine. You know he traffics guns, and we have to make every second count; we must move quickly!" Jerry replied. "The estate is about two miles in length; it would be reasonable to start at the far left and work our way completely around to the far right; there has to be an opening somewhere along the line."

The most difficult part of the journey was traveling through the forestry, working along the boundary lines to prevent getting caught in their tracks and staring into a camera like a deer in headlights. Mike and Jerry's hearts pounded with a hard, fast syncopated rhythm that sounded like the beat of an African drum! At this time, Mike and Jerry were only trying to compile more evidence to use as a bargaining chip! They had no clue which direction this adventure would take them.

Operating solely on faith! They stumbled upon an entrance to the premises, separated by a creek with a small body of water rather quickly; this wasn't necessarily what they had hoped for, but they took what they could get! Immediately after finding a way in, they hurried back to the car to change their muddy shoes and make the necessary readjustments from their wild, improvised blind tour; the tour guides were fantastic!

Unnoticeably, they made their way back to their tables to enjoy the remainder of the concert without casting suspicion.

Mike leaned over in laughter to Carol and said, "We found a way in!"

"Was it difficult to find the entrance?" Carol asked.

"No! In fact, we were extremely lucky! Got a little muddy, but we found a back entrance! The only inconvenience was the barbed wire about four feet high used to prevent the horses from wandering off the property, and we had to cross a dirty creek. It was definitely appalling! In fact, I was almost dismayed to take the chance, but I knew we had to follow through."

Carol's smile of excitement instantly turned into a frown of disparity with inquisitions that spoke to the countless heart-troubling questions and said, "He had his turn! Now it's our time to shine and ridicule his behind! Let's crank up the heat and toast his buns to challenge how much pressure he can take. We're getting a step closer to concluding this ordeal!"

Mike looked over at Jerry and Sherry and nodded with a smile.

Mike then turned back to Carol: "How's the show?"

"It's great! Toni Braxton and Nicki Minaj haven't performed yet! That's who I came to see! She's unpredictable with her sassy swag and off-the-chain style; they're not ready for Nicki! That's my girl!"

Jerry told Sherry, "We found a way in this piece; now all we have to do is creep back in on a later date and take pictures of his stash."

"That's why Mike looked over and smiled; he knew I told you!" Sherry replied.

"That's cool!" she added, preoccupied introspectively thinking about the plan she and Carol had brewing on the side. Mike and Jerry knew nothing about it! A plan was about to be launched; they basically knew all of Mike and Jerry's moves and how to incorporate the two together; the crowd started to scream when Nicki came out on the stage wearing her provocative costume that quite obviously accentuated her incredible body! She was hot!

Chapter 40

At 11 PM, the gala event concluded with the audience taking exclusive advantage of an opportunity to take pictures with the stars; it wasn't every day they got the chance to mix, mingle, and plug their craft!

Mike and Jerry engaged in brief conversation with Mr. Banks before leaving. They mentioned discreetly the dire need for another package within the week!

Banks walked and talked with them, wearing his signature smile implying, "Not a problem! Just put me on prior notice you're coming out that way; I'll have my boys take good care of you! Did you guys enjoy the program? Toni Braxton is hot! I sure would like to take her to bed and make a godfather promise she couldn't refuse."

"I empathize! She's eye candy irresistible to ignore," Mike and Jerry replied.

"I'm excited to hear you guys enjoyed yourselves! I'm sorry, but I have to part company with the two of you to circulate around and extend my appreciation to the other distinguished guests and business partners who helped make this extravaganza come together," Banks said.

"Thank you for the invite!" Mike and Jerry replied.

Mike texted Jerry, "I had Carol get the names of all the elite guests that sat in the first row; I didn't want to take the gamble their conversation wouldn't be detected in the loud crowd by the devices they had inside of them. Moving towards the exit, Mike looked over the crowd to spot Dino and Do Good because they had said earlier they were driving without paying attention to directions; therefore, they clearly didn't know their way home and didn't have GPS to navigate."

Mike and Jerry finally noticed them across the room; it appeared as though Dino and Do Good were looking right at them as well, but sometimes when we think someone is looking at us, they are looking past us.

"Do Good starts pointing at Mike, indicating, 'There are Mike and Jerry over there!'"

They headed toward them to walk out together.

"Let's get out of here; the party's over! Besides, this beer is pouring out of me like a water fountain. Look at this sweat!" Jerry exclaimed.

Mike dropped Jerry and Sherry off at their place. Dino stopped by his house first so Do Good could get his car to take Ebony to the hotel and satisfy their inflamed sexual appetites that had been brewing the entire evening!

Carol pulled out her camera and said to Mike, "Guess who I have pictures of?"

"Who?" Mike asked.

"Toni and her sisters," Carol replied.

"Nope!" Mike said.

"Kenny G!"

"Carol said, "Nope!"

"I know you weren't concerned about getting a picture of the country singer!" Mike stated.

"I snapped pictures of everyone in the front row as you asked, and guess what else?"

"Wait a minute," she replied! Hurrying to turn the radio on to distort their conversation, "I have names of everyone who sat in the front row!"

Mike responded, "So what!"

She implied, "Listen to this," wearing her big infectious smile! "Hold your seat because this is going to blow you away; everyone on the front row are all co-owners of Pleasure Island Resort, which could mean they all play a role in drug distribution, laundering money, and gun trafficking throughout the country!"

"Interruption! You may be onto something. The first thing tomorrow morning, I want you to get that film developed. I need to see the faces of his partners; maybe I can recognize some familiar faces."

The first name jumped off the page was Mr. Ralph Wiggins—the guy we acquired our very first loan from at Boatman's Bank.

"Wait a minute! Here's another familiar face!"

Samantha Willis! "Baby, I have a serious confession; you know I have never lied to you."

"Yes! What are you saying?" Carol asked.

"Well!" he paused for a second. "You remember when I told you?" He stopped there and started communicating through "text" to finish their private conversation about what really happened.

"Oh my God!" Carol exclaimed.

He further texted, "That was about the twentieth time we went on a dangerous mission.

We can also use that as overwhelming evidence to support our legitimate claim for amnesty or immunity from the long laundry list of charges; we were extorted to execute such ungodly sinister acts of violence and other unthinkable crimes because Banks implanted a highly explosive device in our bodies with two other features that recorded everything we said and a GPS that located us no matter where we were. The absolute bottom line equates to 'kill or be killed,' and we certainly didn't want to die.

Early the next morning, she took the film to Walgreens to have it developed. The second they got the film back, Mike quickly thumbed through the stack to see if he recognized anyone; he noticed Starlet Templeton, Banks' girlfriend, and many other faces he couldn't put a name to! He also remembered seeing this person, who turned out to be Mrs. Young, the Honorable Judge of the New York Municipal Court. She was also a co-owner of the resort; two FBI agents named Jeremiah Stinson and George Pollard; they knew for sure they couldn't go to the FBI! They were on his team. But there was always a more appropriate entity: the ATF!

Now that they had this highly explosive information, their fear levels rapidly started to increase, reaching a boiling point of uncertainty about which direction to carry their plan to circumvent or defuse Banks' elaborate scheme and come out on top.

Realizing that the hair-trigger device inside Mike and Jerry had no conscience, she was determined to help in any way possible to make the process work; the jury was out! Baffled which way to turn put everything at odds, so for a while, they decided to give more time to tweaking a tentative game plan for a delicate matter that had been on the table for months, with still no answers to a mind-shattering, crippling paralysis leading to negligence and confusion.

"Lord, please help us find a way, for without You, we're in a tunnel of total darkness and destitution…" Carol said. "We have to seek out the right people to help!" As she thumbed through the pictures in tears, she told Mike, "I love you! I can't continue holding the hurt and pain back. You are the love of my life; it consumes me not being able to help my husband."

"Everything's going to be alright," Mike reassured her. "We just have to take our time and pick our shot when the time is right. At this point, I still have the best poker hand, and it wouldn't be worth challenging his hand right now; it is important that we stay humble and maintain our patience."

"You know, I closely watched you and Jerry at the event, and the two of you looked sort of distant, detached from everything," Carol remarked. "I know it's resting deep on your minds and hearts, but you must not let it stress you out. When you're stressed, you sometimes lose focus and make horribly tragic mistakes along the way that simply can't, under any circumstances, be reversed—like turning the hands back on a clock!"

"I guess with the preoccupation, it's hard to find the funny or fun to shine through. I do understand! It makes me sad as well. In fact, just yesterday, I went to the floor panting, thinking about the crushing blow that happens when you do the wrong thing. I know hustle is in your blood, but it's time to turn that lemon into lemonade. The two of you have skills. You know how to manage and build a house. God has blessed the two of you with the proper tools to take really good care of yourselves for the rest of your lives. Open your eyes. Don't be a fool. In the game, you're only chasing your tail! In the end, you're back to square one."

"Point well taken! I do understand!" Mike replied. "Jerry and I have been going through that same agony and defeat with no available remedy at hand; Jerry seems to take it harder than I do. He's a nervous wreck but conceals it with his jovial attitude; I know better! That's my boy! He could have choked Banks yesterday, but he held his composure tight."

Chapter 41

Three weeks later, the DEA launched a thorough investigation against Dino and Do Good. Word on the streets said they didn't reach kingpin status without the best stuff in town. They didn't only want them; they wanted the connection. They became a demerit for selling drugs on a large scale, coupled with first-degree murder! They were denounced as though they were the worst criminals in the State of New York; they knew where they lived, where three of their dope houses were located, and who was responsible for operations; the investigation was on!

Going back into the archives, they gathered data as far back as the first day they were released from prison. As they continued scrolling down, his hand moved as though it were a magnet on its own course straight to the alleged murders of Corky and "Big Will." This added more fuel to the fire; they were under parole supervision until the year 2024!

The primary connect was the major concern; however, it was a mystery that had them chewing aspirin like junkies every night to curve lingering headaches from pondering in thought. They tried to pick up on a lead; even their gem informants could tap into a source of prevalent information nationwide. These weren't typical local nickel-and-dime boys; this was the mob! Hard "ballers'" sons! These guys had an unlimited rolodex of informational resources nationwide; why do you think Banks' last name is Banks? His dad happened to own multiple banks all named after him: Bank of America, Bank of America, and Bank of America. A billionaire kicking into trillionaire status; an innovative wizard with a slogan: "I'll stop when I drop!" Until such time, I say grind is the name of the game. Pack your lunches to prepare to work late, and always remember: don't stumble along the way.

On April 2, 2023, the FBI secured a search warrant for Dino's arrest for trafficking, which was dismissed with prejudice due to lack of evidence. He was also wanted because a "painter" snitched on him to save his own hide and later ended up in jail on the same tier. That same day, Mike and Jerry were on the highway headed to Banks to "cop" their package: five keys! That was the lick!

On the way back with the cocaine, Mike remembered he had a deadline with the Section Eight Housing Authority to get inspections on ten units prior to submitting vouchers for customers who were in the last inning before their vouchers expired.

He had four days left on the calendar. Jerry dropped Mike off to get his car, and he hurried to City Hall to submit inspection requests, immediately leaving there to head straight to Section Eight to request an inspection on ten properties! He begged for an early appointment to meet the deadline date; he and Mr. Sears had a really good rapport. He inspected the properties the very next day; yes! He had to grease a palm or two or three, but that was okay; he accomplished the goal!

Jerry went to the Henson brothers' house to pick up cash and drop off two of the five keys. When he pulled in front of the Hensons' home, the FBI sat in four unmarked cars, hoping the black BMW belonged to Dino. From many angles, they zeroed in to get a visual on the suspect to confirm they had the right fish on the line. Lieutenant

Fisher replied, "That's our man! We have to be very careful as we move in. We don't want any technical fouls; he won't slip through the cracks today! We've been waiting for this one a long time, gentlemen."

Jerry walked out in a hurry, carrying $500,000 rolled up in a grocery bag. Officer Edwards remarked, "I know he's carrying a large sum of money in that bag!"

Officer Angie Gomez added, "He must have his head in his behind, ostrich style, with the foolish notion no one sees him violating the law!"

Jerry got in his car and drove to the first intersection, impeded by a red light. At that precise moment, four unmarked cars managed to surround his car. Police officers jumped out with guns drawn and FBI badges hanging on their chests like a marquis.

"Get out of the car! Lay face down on the ground!" Officer Edwards commanded. He put him in cuffs and threw him in the back seat of the police car.

"What are we going to find in your car?" Officer Gomez asked as she searched his person. Dino remained silent, biding for a technicality. He knew if a warrant was issued for his home, they still couldn't legally search his car without probable cause; Jerry instantly knew, based on the evidence in his car, he was going to jail!

"Damn!" Jerry thought. "I'm busted!"

The FBI searched the car and found three kilos of cocaine and $500,000 tucked underneath the passenger seat; complacency was his worst enemy! The gatekeeper was caught sleeping on the job. They placed him under arrest and took him into federal custody. The reasons were perfectly clear; they allowed Jerry to drive down the street a little way to get out of view of the Henson brothers' spot.

After Jerry was placed under arrest, they went back to the residence wearing headgear, bulletproof vests, and ninja disguises to execute the search warrant, kicking in and compelling everyone to lay on the floor.

Dino was lucky that day; he was with Ebony at her mother's home. While the search ensued, Dino blurted obscenities! The police told him, "If you don't shut the f*** up, I'll tie your tongue in a knot and shove it down your throat!"

"Man, f*** you! You think you can do whatever you want because you wear a badge!" Dino shouted.

Officer Cobs kicked him in the stomach. Dino attempted to say something, but it came out in a muffled tone, unrecognizable.

"I don't want to hear another word out of you," Officer Cobs said. Officer McGee stood over him and shook his head. He said, "Son, crime is not the answer. You're only chasing your tail, causing yourself grief!"

Ms. Henson and her sixteen-year-old daughter were terrified; Ms. Henson's heart fluttered! She had experienced this one time too many. She was admitted to the hospital ten days earlier and discovered a hole in her heart that needed immediate attention; although the surgery went well, it left her with a very fragile compromised heart condition—now this!

Dino going back to jail hit her like a ton of bricks; the officer couldn't help noticing her gasp for air and needed assistance, so he very reluctantly released her under his conditions as an officer to be careful in dangerous situations! As she stood, quickly grabbing her heart and reaching for the floor to let herself down easy, the officer quickly acknowledged and cushioned her fall as he clutched her under her arms!

The other officers continued transporting evidence out of the dwelling as it was collected to avoid a breach of security using an improper procedure that hampers the state's case through its collection of evidence, technically called a "broken chain of custody…"

They couldn't help noticing her collapse to the floor; in fact, Officer Emanuel Bond helped to break her fall. Before hitting the floor, she was unconscious, flat on her back!

Alexis began to scream uncontrollably; the officer attempted to calm her. I can assure you it wasn't an easy task! The officers kept her inside until the air ambulance arrived. The moment the copter landed, Alexis stormed out the door behind the stretcher.

While this unprecedented activity was going on, the neighbor called Ms. Henson's sister, who lived the next block over, to explain what happened; that she really needed to get there quick; without a guardian, the government has the authority to take the child out of the home and transfer her to juvenile custody until a more appropriate facility can be sought! The only other option was for her big sister to step up to the plate.

Dino gazed out the window of the police car in a dark, intense stare to see who they were wheeling out; he noticed his mother lying on a stretcher, continuing to stare in tears until she was whisked to the hospital ASAP with a massive heart attack. She had previously undergone surgery for a hole in her heart; that second blow was too much!

Chapter 42

Jerry uncomfortably sat in his foxhole, capturing moments when he committed crimes for Mr. Banks; Jerry humbly listened to a voice of reason: "Someday people will understand when you intentionally cause harm to people in any way, it can be devastating in the most unthinkable way; but more importantly, the devastation thrust upon the victim's families left to suffer for the rest of their lives with deep-stricken grief that clogs and hardens the arteries until it snuffs you out." Ms. Henson was unfortunately one exhibit of millions that shines down through the glorious heavenly clouds that serve as the pillows for Christ Jesus, who sacrificed Ms. Henson as His poster child to advocate, "You'll never grasp how much pressure a compassionately tender heart can sustain until it's too late; over! With no recourse to rescind a death certificate!"

Jesus died on the cross for us. What an example setter! He teaches us what not to do, even if it's at the expense of taking one's life to open the eyes of many: "Be always conscious to never bring stress into your home; a place to embellish only with love and joy; we just witnessed how a mother's unconditional love runs straight to the core."

This is the tragic story of miscommunications! An experience that clearly depicts the importance of education being a double-edged sword that takes no hostages; if used improperly, it will open doors unimaginable, like the wind underneath a bird that soars to its highest peak! Without it, you can easily become a danger to yourself and others!

Dino didn't exercise his skills very well. The pieces to his puzzle aren't falling into place anymore; instead, they're falling apart in insurmountable shame and disgrace! The disgrace continues! Later that evening, the ABC and NBC news announced, "A major bust was made today! Six FBI agents raided the Hensons, aka Dino's home; caught with the smoking gun! Two kilos of cocaine stuffed in the ceiling of his bedroom! Sixty thousand dollars in cash and automatic weapons! He was noted for organized crime, and the kingpin act or the anti-terrorism act may be applied.

Two hours earlier, another arrest was made in connection with Mr. Henson! His supplier Jerry was stopped via an FBI investigation that reported he was Dino's supplier; Jerry was arrested with three keys of cocaine, $500,000 in cash, and a .45 automatic handgun! Dino was never one to back down; he never thought about what someone might do to him in jail! Quite the contrary, he was a hot boy! Everybody knew him on the block, and the block was in jail.

The only problem was he was beating the charges; Dino walked into the holdover acting really strange! "What happened, man?" Jerry asked.

"The man kicked in my house about an hour after you left and alleged they found two keys and some fucking money. Soon after they put me in the police car, a helicopter landed. I thought, 'Look at this TV shit. They really are tripping!'"

A few minutes later, a stretcher was wheeled out carrying Dino's mother. She had to be in really bad shape to be rushed by an air ambulance to the hospital.

"Wow, man! I don't know what to say right now! I'm so sorry to hear that happened," Jerry said. "The person responsible for this is a dead man walking."

"When we get out of this pit bull cage, we have to toss those phones; they're contaminated! They've heard too many nightmares about how the police take the chip out and make transformations to another phone. The FBI could taste Mike and Jerry and their 'organic boss of bosses!'"

Dino got out first. He made his one call to get a ride and then tossed it down a sewer. Jerry got caught in a snag! He had an old warrant looming over his head; he had to spend five days in jail to satisfy a speeding ticket and drinking and driving on a void driver's license before posting bail!

On Jerry's first night in jail, he fell from a top bunk and landed on the floor, hurting his hip. The guards heard the boom and the yell for help, but they still took their time before transporting him to the hospital for an examination to determine if he'd fractured his pelvis or if it was just an aching sensation sustained from the hard blow. To Jerry, it felt broken!

The doctor told Jerry, "The x-ray revealed nothing fractured. It hurts because you fell six feet to the floor." He asked the doctor if he could look at the x-rays. This was Jerry's opportunity to find out what was inside; he was curious!

The doctor said, "Sure! Not a problem!"

Mike got off the bed and walked over to view the results, zeroing in on the exact area where the incision was made to see the device implantation! To his surprise, he saw nothing!

He was so excited to learn Banks had played a shrewd psychological game; at least now he knew there was no device. Something told him there was no device because the doctor would have noticed anything unusual in the x-ray! He forgot he had an injury; the doctor gave him pain medication and a crutch, and then the guards returned him back to his cell!

He couldn't wait to get to the phone. When he made it back, there was a long line of people standing in front of him, all having the same dire need to make a connection with someone to get out of jail; although they didn't operate on morals all the time, one man's needs were no more important than the next!

Chapter 43

Two hours passed with deep anticipation; he was next in line, bubbling with diarrhea of the mouth to let the cat out of the bag! The inmate hung up!

Jerry grabbed the phone and dialed as fast as he could to get Mike on the line.

"Operator: Please hang up and try again," Jerry said.

"Damn!" He hung up and dialed again.

On the first ring, Mike answered!

"Hello! Mike, this is Jerry."

"Mike: What's up!"

"Jerry: I got some news off the chain."

"Mike: Come on with that!"

"Jerry: I accidentally fell off the top bunk."

"Mike: Wait a minute! Time out! Are you trying to say, 'You slipped?'"

"Jerry: Come on, man; this is real talk."

"Mike: Okay, man, I was just kidding around with you. What's up?"

"I fell from the top bunk and hurt my hip. I didn't know whether it was fractured or not, so they took me to the hospital for x-rays, and it didn't reveal a fracture or a device planted inside. He manipulated us through an extortion and coercion tactic... He out-hustled us, player, by making us sell his product on the streets; I've never been duked like this. That was a professional 'a league move!'"

"Jerry: He played the game… I only have three days left before my release."

"Mike: I'll be there to see you at visiting hours; but we still can't discuss our best-kept secret about the eye-popping, jaw-dropping overwhelming evidence that will definitely support our strategic game plan; we owe him big time."

Mike was the first person in line at the jail; he was overjoyed to learn Banks had extinguished his power. His joystick was now dysfunctional; Banks had used the device for nearly two years, taking exclusive control over Jerry and Mike's lives, making their lives insanely miserable! A living hell on all burners!

Not an hour after visiting was over, a young man stabbed Jerry with a homemade knife made from a tobacco can transformed into a weapon. Jerry was stabbed in the clippings in the paper! The guards rushed in to pull him out of the tier to get him to the hospital as fast as they could! He died crossing the threshold to the operating room; he met his demise at the hands of a stranger who turned out to be Anthony, Big Will's younger brother.

Big Will and Corky were killed together at the hands of Dino and Do Good; they were employed by Jerry. The police couldn't quite put the pieces together; but as a courtesy to a player, "the streets" was Anthony's playground! The information the police couldn't obtain was hopscotch for him. He roamed the streets, ate the streets, breathed and drank the street where his DNA ran 24/7.

He swore if he ever ran into anybody connected or remotely responsible for his brother's murder, it was a death sentence, going straight for the jugular without a hint of discretion! Anthony found out through a source in jail that Jerry was Dino and Do Good's connect when Big Will and Corky got killed.

Lives are affected in ways unimaginable by everything we do, whether good or bad; only God knows!

Mike knew he had to "proceed with caution." Otherwise, the red light machete bandit's slogan, "It's like that," would haunt him!

Mike had no idea Jerry was killed less than an hour after leaving! It wasn't until he met with Do Good to drop off a package that he received a call from his sister.

"Sherry: crying frantically, trying to explain Jerry was stabbed to death. He died before they could get him out of the cell block!"

Mike, shocked in disbelief that his best friend was killed within hours of leaving, exclaimed, "How can this be?" Now Mike was really angry, tossing things! Revenge poured profusely through his veins! A catastrophe masterminded by the catalyst himself, Mr. Banks! It was time to step up to the plate.

Mike handed Do Good two keys. "It's urgent that we call a meeting; there is something I want to share that will bring us all a big payday. I do understand our families have to be fed, and life continues to move forward no matter what. Your mother had Jerry put away presidentially. Unfortunately, Jerry lost his parents in a car accident. He'll have the best going-home celebration. That's my boy! I love him! Plus, lawyers got to be paid."

Mike spoke boldly, knowing there was no device to persuade him not to overstep certain boundaries. They were in the resounding eighth inning with two outs favoring Banks. Oh, but the tables had taken a dramatic turn; his pitching had just blown out without a second string coming to the rescue. It wasn't funny when the rabbit had the gun! "Play ball! I'll definitely call you guys with a time and place to go over the details," Mike said, referring to Throw Down and his boys. "I have to be going! Sherry and Carol need me home to console them. This day I'll never forget. They're devastated by this tragedy! I'll catch you later!"

"It's going to be alright; please believe that! We're going to make it happen! That's what real soldiers do! Be at peace, my brothers!" Do Good replied.

Mike said, "Perseverance!" He hopped in his car and drove off, thinking the fifty thousand Banks had given him for Jerry's bond now had to be used for funeral expenses, thanks to Banks. He had a cataract badly distorting his vision. He didn't take into account Mike or Jerry could possibly fall and get hurt requiring x-rays. Mike didn't personally care what he was up against. He only knew payback wasn't going to be nice.

He got home to find Carol and Sherry sobbing over the loss of Jerry, both assuming Banks had a hand in his demise. He did this to keep him quiet. The girls stepped up and became captains and lieutenants in this mission to get revenge for Jerry and for Dino and Do Good's mom. Mike and his boys were just pawns on Banks' chessboard; Carol and Sherry knew how to fight a shrewd battle that would leave Banks spinning in a daze. It would take him a lifetime to figure out the suspenseful drama coming next.

Chapter 44

The next day after the bust, Mike boldly walked into the police department at noon to speak with officers from the D.E.A, Alicia, Emanuel, and Lt. Kathy Walsh. As he entered the office, he slowly canvased the room with a quiet stare at everyone in attendance of this big gala event. "I held the prize key to make the cartels buckle to their knees and beg for mercy!" he thought, amazed. The room was congested with bomb experts, Chinese physicians specializing in intense critical situations prepared to perform surgery, and X-ray technicians with portable labs to determine where the bomb was located in the body. Once he was X-rayed, the D.E.A had a helicopter on standby to whisk him to the hospital for surgery.

"Let the interrogations begin!" he thought. He had to be on his toes at that point! This was crucial! Watching cop shows on TV, he knew that if he didn't cooperate fully with them, he wouldn't have to undergo the witness protection program, which he felt no need to pursue under the circumstances. Banks knew nothing. Plus, he wasn't forced into a witness protection program; the primary concern was to provide enough information that warranted a conviction. With that, he knew what to disclose and what not to. Officer Walsh gestured with her hand for Michael to have a seat; immediately, they started clicking buttons, "texting" questions nonstop. It was awfully difficult to keep up with the line of questioning as everyone in the room animatedly tapped their cell phones with back-to-back questions; it reminded one of the rapid-firing cameras that took a picture as fast as you could press the button!

"Michael, you do realize you are here because you and your friend Jerry were connected to the mob and forced to take on certain responsibilities that were contrary to the law," Officer Alicia stated. "We assume criminal acts were undertaken consistent with murder, drugs, gun distribution, money laundering, sales of high explosives and their usage, extortion, and more. My condolences go out to you for the loss of your friend. But to be quite honest, cutting right through to the chase, in order for us to help get you cleared of this, you must lower your guards and cooperate; you must tell everything you know to prevent these guys from slipping through a crack! Power is knowledge, and we're trying to protect you!"

Emanuel attempted his scare tactic: "Let me ask you! Is Banks capable of murder?"

"Yes! I also understand I'm bound by his clutches. Other than that, he has absolutely no reason to suspect I set him up," Mike replied.

Kathy intervened, "Through our investigation, it has been learned there were daytime shots of you and Banks chatting; our lip readers reported they'd looked into some pretty interesting conversations. Incriminating, at best!"

"Many people in bad situations come to us with gross misleading information with the intention of playing a game of cat and mouse; in those kinds of cases, we simply cannot provide new identities or new locations. It's almost always a tragedy when people play with their lives like it's a carnival ride! Eventually, the mob catches up to them, force-feeding them into a human meat grinder; blood, flesh, and bones pour out the other end, resembling hamburger meat sifted out with heavy blood content! Now, what additional information can you provide us with that we haven't already secured from your wife and sister?"

Emanuel added, "As you can see, we have a dynamic team here ready to assist you through this frightening ordeal; but first, we have to get X-rays taken to determine exactly where the device is located and the possibility of its removal! The reason I used the term 'possibly' is that the department did not find the remote control to the device in its search, and tampering with that device could set off a negative signal." The text messaging continued while the X-ray tech set up his apparatus.

Kathy said, "I can imagine the emotions that run rampant knowing you have dynamite explosives inside you that could blow at any second! I know you're on pins and needles!"

Mike took a stance straight, with no chase! He knew they were going to assert their authority like the big bad wolf, assuming he was afraid. But that didn't shake him. "I was crushed! I felt like the atom split in half, with the most intricate part belonging to someone else, leaving me with an empty shell and the ability to propel in the direction they wanted. I had become a human puppet, deeply frustrated and depressed, knowing someone had dominion over my life!" He went further to explain, "My wife and sister spoke with you yesterday, and what was explained to me is that they gave you more than enough evidence to take these guys down. I don't think it's necessary to tell you everything we were compelled to do in exchange for our lives. That'll only put us more in harm's way because to prove these 'allegations,' firsthand information must be supplied if available, and I'm not trying to testify on nobody's stand against no family well known as killers! Please don't think I'm trying to be belligerent!"

"Michael, I sincerely empathize with you! But be assured we have the power invested to suppress anybody's identity based purely on that possibility alone; we know you could be 'signing a death certificate to have your life and your family extinguished.' The judge and prosecutor completely understand the exact nature of your situation and by no means do they practice sacrificing a life just to find the answers to the truth; they would never negligently drop the ball and expose a witness's identity or his anonymity. Trust me! Whatever you say here stays here. It will remain strictly confidential, with the promise the chain of custody will not be broken or compromised under any circumstance," Officer Alicia assured him.

Mike encountered a fleeting thought that determined the direction he should take. He knew the government had no friends; they would turn on you in a second. Their sole objective was to catch the criminals at large, not make friends with them. So he decided to continue with caution and not expose his royal flush; they only knew what he told them! The federal government was studious and very tricky! Notorious for breaching agreements; especially when half of the force was on the take and the other was a work in progress! It was about that almighty dollar! Information only walks if money talks! The X-ray technician indicated to Kathy they were ready to take pictures to pinpoint exactly where the device was planted; through his X-ray, he discovered nothing!

Kathy approached Mike and gave him the best news he had received in quite some time. "As she walked toward Mike, he stared with an expression of curiosity, 'Can this bomb be removed?'"

"I have some extremely good news for you!"

"What's the good news?" Mike looked into her sensual eyes.

"The X-ray technician found nothing unusual!"

Mike was performing an act! He put his hands over his face and dropped his head, thanking the Lord for not putting him through more than he could bear. He held his head down almost the entire time she explained how they were wedged in a strongly woven web that was devastating; the harder they struggled, the more the pain increased! The pain, the exclusive control, and the suspense combined were too much to bear!

The rootless Mr. Banks studied psychology and became the master of deception! He obviously gave them an antistatic, as Sherry mentioned, and pretended he implanted disgusting devices inside them that made them cringe with chill bumps and potentially suffer cardiac arrest. "He sold you to think through the power of suggestion that a proverbial device had been inserted at your pancreas with the premise you must obey his every command!" Alicia exclaimed.

"Wow! You were definitely at his mercy! I can only imagine the nightmarish experience he's put you through. Your family! The loss of your friend, your friend's mother; the daredevil stunts you had to do to satisfy his insane appetite. To say the least, that's a very expensive price to pay for sticking your hands in that hot, sticky pot of stew! We have them now, and they won't be getting out anytime soon," Mike stated.

"You talk a good game, but these guys are all out on a million dollars bond each," Mike replied.

"Yes, they're out on bond, but we had conversations with the D.A. and judge respectively, requesting Banks and his boys be taken back off bail and recharged under the Rico or Kingpin statute for organized crime! Drugs, extortion, gun running, and explosives; O.J. Simpson's attorney said so eloquently, 'If the gloves don't fit, you must acquit.' Well, sorry, these gloves all fit; we have all the correct sizes tucked away in our evidence file!"

Finally, Mike raised his head to reveal the enormous emotional blow he'd sustained through his sobbing, tearful eyes and trembling voice that had no control switch. Alicia empathically handed him a napkin to dry his tears; at the same time, Emanuel and Kathy cordially extended their appreciation to the X-ray technicians and escorted them to the door.

Kathy and her team were not about to risk any technical violations on appeal for having unofficial parties in the interrogation room while a witness was being interrogated! The X-ray technicians both nodded their heads in gratitude and shook their hands as they quietly exited the room. Alfred, the X-ray tech, told his friend departing the room, "What an interesting ordeal! I've never witnessed anything of this nature."

His colleague responded, "That's spooky! I'll bet his vital signs are over the edge! He was riding a roller coaster with no breaks or padding to cushion the blow against the impact once it crashed!" They continued chatting as they walked through the long hallway, finally exiting the jail.

"A Mike, tell me the story from your perspective. Can you do that? Your wife and sister mimicked you well, but it's not like getting it straight from the horse's mouth. Straight, no chase; a real swaggalicious story! Don't misunderstand me! I feel you! I clearly understand your reason for not wanting to disclose incriminating information that may deadlock you in a situation compelling your testimony in court; but you must know we have a way of finding information. Our sources are unlimited! For instance, flight records, hotel visits, restaurants, and people engaged."

"We have crafty ways of maneuvering our way into the privacy of your home, sitting down at your dinner table and absorbing the 411! We're professionals at jarring memories to secure priceless information!" Mike took a deep breath and then began telling the incredible story from the very first day, with exceptions to the murders. He talked about how he and Jerry were the muscle that made sure drugs dropped on time, and how guns and other weapons were distributed to vendors with new business clients' expectations daily. "We also had the responsibility of making sure all the runners for the mob in the Bronx, Harlem, and Brooklyn were always in pocket. I learned through the mob why maintaining a consistently good product is paramount in the business! Clients won't take a chance going anywhere else because they know they can get that good, good!"

Two hours later, Mike finally finished his story, leaving everyone speechless now knowing the real man behind the mask!

"Banks is incredibly witty; he is so persuasive he could convince a three-legged cat to walk into a dog pound filled with pit bulls and dare set up a card table, beckoning the most treacherous dogs to challenge him in a game of bid whiz!" Emanuel exclaimed.

"Unbelievable! Mike, we really appreciate all the information you've provided us with. If you think your life is not in danger at this point, that's your call. We are not here to judge or force you and your family into a witness protection program. That is strictly your call; it can be very dangerous! However, while this investigation is ongoing, we'll be looking in on you from time to time to make sure you and your family are okay. Please don't hesitate to give us a call if there's any intrusion or if you get a gut feeling your life is in imminent danger; don't try to go it alone!"

"Don't worry! I know how to defuse my situation now that I know there's no device inside me; I'm not implying retaliation either. Banks has been paid in full! As far as I'm concerned, Jerry's life was his last and final payment! It's 3:45 on a Friday! Interrogation's over!" He shook their hands and politely exited the room; walking down the corridor, he contemplated, "Where do I go from here?" With ten kilos of cocaine on ice and twenty-five pieces of property all under section eight housing, should he take the high road and work his rental properties aggressively, continuing to grow in the real estate industry? Or should he have his cake and eat it too, maintaining the real estate and continuing to grind in the streets with that ten kilos, which would take him to the next level? The jury was still out! He was at a deadlock! The low road was something to consider; the thought certainly smelled delicious but could be a deadly deceptive scent that could cause greater turmoil!

This was his final call, and he had to view his life from a realistic perspective and exercise his intellect over emotion to get the best results to navigate his way through! Still confused! That following Sunday, he and Carol went to church for the first time in the past two years. Mike was drawn to the church to find answers to a difficult tug of war that played in his head; stay tuned to see if the church was his divine intervention or if a demonic spirit took charge. Sometimes, making poor decisions is based on the company you keep. That bug in your ear! For instance, if you're in recovery, the smart thing to do is not hang out with the same corrupt company, visit the same places that pose a trigger, or take grave risks by being in direct contact with things like drugs, syringes, guns, and in some cases, money that can be the primary cause of a relapse.

Ten kilos are a lot to pour down a drain! Likewise, living a normal lifestyle with twenty-five properties is also a tremendous sacrifice; it is an awful lot to pour down a drain as though it has minimal or no value at all! While Mike was thinking about what he was going to do with the rest of his life, Banks, on the other hand, wasn't having as much fun in thought!

Banks and his boys ambushed behind the judge's chambers! That following Monday morning at 9:00 AM, Banks and his mobster family had to appear in court; they had no idea the charges were about to change to a more severe state. Their bonds would all be revoked, leaving them detained in custody pending trial without the possibility of securing bail, cash, or property; they were all considered a flight risk and had gained an enormous amount of attention across the nation.

The judicial system was put in a vice grip and forced to apply pressure. This case took a course of its own. The notorious pit bull mobsters didn't deserve a free pass. Lockup was the only answer!

Banks and his mob family walked into the courtroom wearing Armani suits, filling the court with no seats for outsiders or the media; the entire courtroom was literally monopolized! The D.A. knew this was going to happen! Mobster cases always generate rough edges, so he requested backup sheriffs days in advance! He also knew the tricky part would be maintaining control in the courtroom once bonds were revoked. So the judge decided to lure each of them out of the courtroom after approaching the bench to read their new charges under the Rico statute, with the understanding that the new mandatory DNA law mandates, "DNA must be secured from any person charged with a violent offense before a release on bail!"

The judge entered the courtroom. "Everybody rise for the Honorable Judge McShane. You may be seated!"

"Good morning! I'm going to do a roll call. If you didn't hear your name called on the docket, it will be read a second time later. Furthermore, today is arraignments! Arraignment hearings are conducted to determine the following: The offense charged, how you plead on the offense, new court dates, and appointing attorneys if you cannot afford one! Which brings to mind, you are not considered a 'pauper' if you are currently on bail; once the charges were read,

Robert Banks, Alex Delgoti, and Larry Trout were escorted through the back door of the courtroom by a sheriff!

Waiting on the other side of the doors for Banks, Alex, and Larry's surprise was a team of sheriffs ready to put them in cuffs while the sheriff working the court returned to get the rest of them; they had absolutely no idea what was taking place behind closed doors! They couldn't afford a breach in security through an episode of disorderly conduct or an outburst that might trigger a loss of control in this courtroom; too many high triggers could cause a serious eruption! Charlie Pesiea, AKA "Big Crush," had to make his presence known! "Did you guys hear what she just said about DNA? I'm not giving any freaking DNA!" The sheriff cautiously walked over to get his attention. "One more outburst like that, and your DNA won't be important; I'll place you under arrest; then guess what, young man, we'll get that DNA, so don't let your tongue cut you."

As the sheriffs walked away, he uttered under his breath, "You'll never find your way to my house with my DNA! I'll gladly give you someone else as soon as we smoke his ass out of the woodwork." Just before they could call Tommy Brooks, AKA "Big Fun," he had to follow suit with!

"I have places to go and people to see; I don't have time for this nonsense! My dinner's getting cold!" Judge McShane exclaimed. "Order in my courtroom!" She continued to call them one at a time until finished. Gary Stemson's name was next on the docket, followed by Big Frank Gurshman, Little John Cezaar, the Widow Maker Catherine Anastaha, and Charlie Winters! The mission was successfully accomplished with her staff's assistance.

The judge announced, "If you're waiting on your party to return from DNA testing, I want to advise you they were transferred to the jail facility to be tested, and the nurse's station closed an hour ago; therefore, no one's available to draw the blood work, and unfortunately, they're going to be detained until the blood work has been completed! Thank you, and have a nice day!" She rose from her seat and started to exit the courtroom when someone in the audience yelled out, "This is bullshit! We've been tricked!"

The evening news dropped the bombshell that startled the mob!

Channel 4 Samuel Dawson Reporting: "Today at the New York federal court building, the biggest case in the nation's history just erupted like a volcano. Ten mob family members were all arraigned, and new charges were filed; the court was under extreme caution when the ten gangsters were arraigned. They had to use a very unique tactic to lure the mobs into a vulnerable place to take them down without incident and place them in custody! They are back in custody with charges of organized crime under the Rico statute for first-degree murder, drugs, guns, and high explosives accompanied by eerie intrusive extortion tactics that have destroyed many lives stretching from coast to coast."

Mike and Carol were watching it on the evening news. It was a huge relief to witness the arrests; now that they were in custody, all the chaos and confusion Mike felt had dissipated. The only person who knew about him and Jerry, to his knowledge, was Banks, Samantha, Starlet Templeton, the two Mexicans, and Ralph Wiggins! He must not realize that the Great Wall of China had ears and people talked! Boy, was he in for a big surprise!

Meanwhile, Throw Down, M One, Do Good, Dino, and the rest of the death squad were laid back, peeking on a natural high, sitting on a couple of kilos, resting, and playing with the young ladies with irresistible "swaggalicious" assets that made your mouth water! It made you stop and take a shot at spending time on the DL.

Banks and his boys, on the other hand, were a nervous wreck, wrapped in a mystery no one knew the answers to, plus stuck in jail with no way out! Their first instinct was to use that one guaranteed phone call to see if the chess pieces were still maneuverable or if it was checkmate. The informant's identity was the essential key. They had to get to him fast! Banks was one of the few people who could link the dots. But it would take some incredible pressure to crack his bank open.

He reflected back to his childhood at age thirteen when he and a distant acquaintance attended the same school but never had any of the same classes. He wanted to be friends to avoid bullying, or maybe genuinely good friends. They committed a burglary that ended on a very tragic note; they had stolen two guns from a home: a twenty-five automatic and a .22 pistol! His friend gave him the option to choose which gun he wanted; he chose the twenty-five automatic. His friend handed him the gun, and he decided to play a game, turning his back for a second to download the clip. He told his friend, "I should kill you." He knew bullets had been taken from the clip, so he told him to go ahead and pull the trigger.

Banks pulled the trigger not knowing a bullet rested in the chamber. The click of the trigger was the only sound expected, but to his surprise, the gun went off, startling him. His eyes popped, and his jaw became unhinged, leaving him in awe with his mouth wide open in tears. When his friend fell to the ground from the gunshot hitting him dead center in the chest, Banks made an attempt to move him so he would be comfortable while waiting for the hospital. He was paralyzed from the waist down.

He was later apprehended for the burglary and sentenced to serve time in a juvenile boy's home along with his friend, who was paralyzed for playing precariously with a handgun! Kids didn't know about guns; they were just infatuated with their power! That was really hard for Banks because, first, he accidentally shot his friend, and then he moved him; he harbored the thought to this day that he could be the one who caused him to be paralyzed!

Banks momentarily snapped out of his trance, contemplating the separation from his friends. They were put on different tiers to prevent communication. At that point, the D.E.A. commenced their "league game of divide and conquer" by sifting out the weakest link. Once separated, the mind began to explore many places, entertaining many possibilities! When they put chisel to chain, vigorously cranking the grinding wheel with no letting up, they planted the subliminal seed that they could serve the rest of their lives in prison if they didn't cooperate with the authorities!

"We've been tricked like stooges! There's got to be a way out!" Banks exclaimed. He contacted his attorneys, and all they could say was, "Sit tight. We have to do the math on this one; Judge McShane is not letting up!"

At this point, everybody was considered a flight risk based on the nature of the allegations. The judge was animatedly determined not to suffer a backlash of criticism for allowing bail to members of the mob with high-profile charges of organized crime looming over their heads! She'd just let a rapist out a week earlier who had two prior heinous rape convictions. He was released on a technicality, then raped and killed a sixteen-year-old waiting on the bus early that Saturday morning on her way to her aunt Helen's to go job hunting! McShane couldn't afford a media circus!

Banks' attorney came to visit with more bad news. "The motion was denied to compromise the confidentiality of the informant to challenge credibility," he said. "Although it is well-settled law that most informants are under duress and will say anything to get out of jail, the motion was still denied based on overwhelming physical evidence and the thought of potential physical harm that may incur based on reputations!"

Banks went into a twilight state, thinking, "Anything can happen at this point!" He called his fiancée, Starlet Templeton, who, with her unfiltered tongue that spoke freaky straightforward in a "swaggalicious" style that made her really sexy, told him, "All your accounts and assets are frozen, and the resort is under potential seizure by the federal government." He silenced himself, turning the pages back in remembrance of all the wonderful times; it was even more excruciating knowing his organization affiliates were learning what had happened and abandoning him because he exemplified misrepresentation and disgrace!

Getting the bad news made his pressure boil and his head ache severely; his stomach suffered a familiar cramp that vividly reminded him of how he felt when he occasionally insisted on not consuming cocaine; his nose ran like a faucet without a washer.

Before he could hang up, Starlet heard him panting for breath and seemed very disoriented because his responses were incoherent. The phone dropped as he went to his knees, gasping for air. Banks died from pancreatic cancer that he knew absolutely nothing about! He thought his excruciating stomach cramps were attributed to his extensive cocaine usage. Anytime he encountered pain, he would assume it was just a need for a hit and went straight for the cooker! Of course, that was a personal assessment!

Chapter 45

Now everyone was scrambling, trying to figure out what could have happened; thoughts were turning in everybody's heads that someone in the jail had given him a drug overdose that took him out!

Later, the autopsy report revealed he had suffered pancreatic cancer that was in its fourth stage and hadn't been treated with chemotherapy. Starlet immediately hung up and called Ralph Wiggins. When the phone rang, he was pacing the floor back and forth, worried he would get a knock on the door that would land him in jail. He was looking in the window of his career as the owner of several banks, having extended a loan to Mike and Jerry to purchase real estate with Banks as the co-signer on the loan. He knew the feds left no stone unturned, and it was only a matter of time before he was called in for questioning.

Finally, he picked up the phone after about eight rings. "Hello!"

"Hi, Ralph! This is Starlet!"

"Hi!"

"I have some really crushing news. Robert called, and as I was sharing some bad news I received in the mail that explained the federal government had frozen his assets and all of his accounts!"

"They placed a lien against the resort! I guess they didn't want him to use it as collateral. Hold yourself together for this: while I was talking to him, I heard him panting for breath, and then he went silent. He expired while we were talking."

"I'm going to let the dust settle before I have my attorneys contest the lien on the property, considering my name and Samantha's is endorsed as co-owners. The only thing that kept me and Samantha out of the picture is the fact that we reside in different states, and there's no reason for them to assume we had any knowledge. I'll fly in tonight so we can make funeral arrangements and discuss you managing the property. It's sad, but Robert lived a very precarious lifestyle of partying, popping his crystal liquor, and running lines of the best cocaine in town. He had the best of everything!"

One hour earlier, members of the mob on all tiers got word that Banks died while on the phone. With his demise, seven out of ten mob members were seriously contemplating "getting down first"! They figured if they snitched first, they could probably get a really good deal.

That night at lockdown, the guards made their rounds, doing a head count. Notes strangely emerged from nowhere, conveying that mob members were flipping over like pancakes. Kathy, Alicia, and Emanuel all instantaneously rose from their seats when the news came across the wire!

"Patience will break a jawbreaker! I knew time was in our favor!" Kathy exclaimed.

"That's what usually happens when you separate criminals during an investigation; it's not hard convincing a thug that his partner caved in if they're not allowed to communicate!" Alicia added. "Especially when the double-edged sword represents death or a life sentence in the Department of Corrections!"

Emanuel replied, "I beg to differ! If Banks didn't shockingly clock out without a sign of failing health, we may not be as lucky. We would have had a relentless struggle on our hands that could have ended in a bloodbath unimaginable!"

"You've got a good point, but realistically the ice is broken! You may as well strap yourself in because we're getting ready to ride this baby out!"

"Now's the time for us to get over to the jail and tightly ratchet every bolt down securely to establish a classic prima facie case that'll permanently put a crease in their pants! You have to realize they are falling apart at the seams. Their once solid conduit has collapsed with huge holes resembling tuberculosis gone untreated."

At the same time Kathy and her team went to the jail, Throw Down was out cruising the Boulevard, checking his traps, making sure production got the green light stamp of approval. Throw Down and Do Good were caught by the red light; he was taken totally by surprise by the red light machete bandit who approached his car while waiting for the light to change! He finally rose from underneath the covers of darkness to make yet another permanent mark of terror that haunted society! Did anyone imagine this unexpected visit was inevitable? What do you think happened?

He hopped around the car, slamming his machete one more time, catching a flashy youngster at the intersection; he got his bracelet, ring, and watch, along with an 8-ball he held in his hand. The nightmare continued.

Do Good was obviously doing him, flirting with the honeys and working his way through the maze in a daze, wondering if he'd make it successfully. The insatiable glitter and glamour were overwhelmingly infectious. It made him cling to his dream of someday being on top, which was none other than a fleeting dream filled with gaping holes he could easily fall through at any given time.

His cell phone rang, breaking his concentration as he tried to screen all calls before answering! He noticed Dino's call and attempted to answer! When he picked up, the call disconnected! It happened regularly, so he thought nothing of it and waited for him to call again; maybe he was interrupted and had to check a trap or a booty call.

Precarious was the lifestyle "Do Good" portrayed, knowing the dangers involved, but that didn't seem to matter; that was what made his adrenaline pulsate to get that euphoria; it made him feel like he was somebody! "Grind for life" was tattooed on his chest! Ride or die was the motto he lived by!

An hour earlier, Starlet Templeton was seriously contemplating how to cunningly assume ownership or play a major role as she quietly thumbed through a plan of action in her mind's eye. While gazing in admiration out the huge picture window in her office, she was rendered a showcase view of the most sensational landscape that extended clear across the estate! She was deeply engulfed in a thought that reminded one of the hawk that sees its prey miles away, night or day, and is always ready to strike! She was phenomenally witty with an extraordinary recipe that allowed her to always come out on top! She was the best independent top investigator in the country, which is why she was a threat to contenders; she was the only one who knew who informed on Banks.

Having personal relations with a key player in the D.E.A. certainly gave her the edge. She had fringe benefits that allowed her to break any chain of custody in the department; it enabled her to decrypt the informant's real names as they were changed to protect confidentiality. Obviously, she had a personal agenda to suppress the information; just you wait and see.

Her random thoughts shifted back and forth to the last conversation she had with Banks, envisioning him helplessly falling to his knees, dropping the phone to the floor. The phone rang, breaking a priceless moment. Starlet picked it up. "Ralph!"

"Hi!"

"Can you hold for a minute? I'm getting Samantha on the line." Samantha picked up.

"Starlet and I have you on this conference call. We need to discuss Starlet running the resort." After Ralph's conversation with the two of them via telephone conference, it astounded Starlet to learn she was the only candidate mentioned to manage the resort. That certainly quenched her thirst!

"Starlet, we'll discuss the details later; I just want to inform you to put on your new hat as C.E.O. of that enterprise."

Through her practice, Starlet had gained nationwide notoriety for getting the "last word" for a very good reason; she was extremely irresistibly sexy, witty, and a terrifyingly relentless tiger unleashed when going after what she wanted! She continued grappling with the unthinkable loss of Robert! One intriguing man with fascinating ideas; Starlet yielded at nothing to accomplish her quest! She was the next kingpin to inherit Banks' empire and his ruthless ways as the pressure peaked to a boiling point!

Throw Down and the rest of the young DL "Ballers" continued daily, beating the streets, rolling out "slinging dope," banging hoes, and dropping penicillin daily just in case they caught a crab! "M One" had an anxiety attack and went his separate way. He thought he was on top of the world like Tony Montana until he stuck his nose under that white dress! Taking that nosedive blew his mind; he managed to acquire heart disease and extremely high irregular heart rhythms. One early morning, he woke up, rolling over to his plate of cocaine, ran a line of that white bitch, and died.

The police continued shutting down dope houses as a discouraging tactic, but they were hungry beasts always wanting more; they'd lock them up for drug trafficking and gun charges, but no matter what, they were back on the block later that evening on bail, pending a court date! It was a vicious cycle! Lawyers violated the code of ethics, selling first-class nightmare stories to their clients about how the judge desperately wanted to send dealers to prison for a lifetime! How prosecutors would not back off the fifteen-year offer! They didn't think going to jail was a possibility if they kept greasing the right palms; that perception became a trigger that encouraged them to continue taking grave risks, making money at the expense of burying themselves to satisfy a lawyer's hidden motives called "greed" to drain his client's pockets dry by charging for continuous appeals to prolong a penalty phase!

They knew they weren't going to trial and at some point had to enter a plea agreement, yet the borrowed time didn't seem to matter. In the midst of the turmoil, they opened Club "N Trapment" and a chain of restaurants; they couldn't boil water correctly, but they were smart enough to use the Henry Ford concept: "They supplied the concept and hired someone to execute the plan of action." It sounded ridiculous coming from a bunch of eighth-grade dropouts, especially given the police were on their tail 24/7! Once their lawyers exhausted their remedies, they'd end up in prison, not able to buy a box of crackerjacks!

Now they were calling home, agonizing over poor mom who'd been on a fixed income for the past ten years. "Momma, I need you to put money on my books so I can go to the commissary to spend!"

Until one day, waking up and looking into the mirror while brushing their teeth, they accidentally discovered age had rapidly crept upon them; now they were much older with virtually no security blanket. Unfortunately, things got worse because they decided to run the streets without an inkling of responsibility! Living off the fat of the land! What a life!

Officer Kathy Walsh always said when foolishly chasing unrealistic dreams like the many Bonnie and Clyde stories, oftentimes a vision inevitably got distorted through a desperation to stockpile money, which caused them to forget there was a rigorous manhunt and investigations going on that could put them away for the rest of their lives. In an uncanny kind of way, they apparently thought no one saw them, as though they were invisible yet standing center stage, demonstrating the worst choreography under Big Brother's super lens cameras, with the most gorgeous lighting ready for the whole world to see their unscrupulous imperfections accompanied by an infamous act of stupidity! Living like an ostrich! There were thousands upon thousands of kids extorted and severely abused by dead-end institutionalized convicts who sat in prison cages for dinosaur years waiting for a vulnerable prey to wander their way!

The End!